ACKNOWLEDGE & HEAL

A WOMEN-FOCUSED GUIDE TO PTSD

VIRGINIA CRUSE & KATIE SALIDAS

ISBN: 978-1-7348067-2-4

First Publication date August 26, 2022

Published by: Military Counseling Center San Antonio, PLLC
MilitaryCounselingSA.com
www.TheSoldiersBlog.com

Interior Layout and Cover Design by: Rising Sign Books
RisingSignBooks.com
KatieSalidas.com

For inquiries contact: militarycounselingsa@gmail.com

Ladies:

What you're experiencing is a normal reaction to trauma.
What happened was not your fault.
You are not damaged.
You deserve to heal.

INTRODUCTION

Hey, Lady -

So, we don't know each other. I only know that you have picked up this book and, for the moment, you're reading it. I appreciate that; there are few things I value more than the counsel of wise women. After writing The Soldier's Guide to PTSD, I heard from many women - both Veterans and civilians - who felt validated once they were armed with the facts. These women knew in their gut that they were experiencing symptoms of PTSD and could not find help. Sometimes, their doctors and mental health professionals would not listen to them.

Unfortunately, I know a bit about that. In 2008, after my third deployment to Iraq, I was at my worst with my own PTSD and my boss directed me to see a psychiatrist. This was at a military treatment facility and the psychiatrist was an active duty military officer, a male colonel. I was overwhelmed, suicidal, and in an extremely vulnerable position. I knew something was seriously wrong with my mental health, and I didn't understand what was happening to me. It was frightening.

I talked with this psychiatrist for the better part of an hour. I answered his questions and poured my heart out. At the end of our time he said to me, "Virginia, there's nothing I can do to help you if you can't be honest with me." I was bewildered. He further qualified his statement and said, "we all know women don't serve in combat, and I can't help you if you won't tell me the truth."

I wish I were making this up. This psychiatrist labeled me with a personality disorder and he completely dismissed my experience. I felt like I was kicked while I was already down. Adding insult to injury, I was kicked by another service member who was supposed to have my back.

I remember that day very well even though I was drinking a lot back then; the feeling of betrayal cut deeply. I internalized this hurt and thought seriously about giving up. In that moment, I realized that if I didn't figure out how to help myself I was literally going to die, either from insanity or by my own hand. I enrolled in graduate school and, thirteen years later, here I am talking to you.

I've talked with hundreds of clients since then and discovered that my experience is not a one-off, and, unfortunately, this goes beyond the Veteran community. Often, women's experiences are dismissed, belittled, and invalidated – and even more so for women of color or women who identify as a member of the LGBTQIA+ community. It's not okay.

Ladies: we absolutely have to know our symptoms better than anyone else – this includes our doctors or our therapists. We must be able to advocate for ourselves and sound smart doing it. I'm convinced that when we know the facts about PTSD we make more informed choices and get better faster.

This message is important, which is why I partnered with Katie Salidas to write this Women's Guide. Katie has a way of communicating that is beyond my scope, and I would be crazy not to tap into her expertise.

When we asked for feedback for The Soldier's Guide in 2021, many women that I love and respect told us that The

Soldier's Guide has great information, but the tone was too harsh and the jargon too specific. We listened and changed course.

That doesn't mean that this book will be comfortable, though. PTSD is an unpleasant topic and people don't like to talk about it. I get that, but that's not good for us. Your life is at stake, Lady, and I intend to be as straightforward as I know how. We're going to talk about suicide, gaslighting, depression, relationships, and more.

Because I'm one of those therapists who came to the profession later in life, I'm not here to waste time. I'm going to teach you everything I wish I knew before I walked into that colonel's office. I know PTSD is exhausting, and I realize you may not be up to reading a book. But maybe you could try this one. We'll keep it short.

Yours Sincerely,

Virginia Cruse

TABLE OF CONTENTS

CHAPTER 1 PTSD RUMORS

Rumors that are absolutely not true
and mess with your head!

There is a lot of information out there about PTSD, but most of what's out there is not user friendly. That's because most what is out there is written by clinicians for clinicians using psychobabble that reads like IKEA furniture building instructions. It's meant to help those who help others, and while well-intentioned, it isn't easily digestible for the rest of us.

The Skinny

Post means "after."

Trauma is exposure to death, serious injury, or sexual violence. Trauma happens to you; it's not something wrong with you.

Stress is your body's psychological and physical reaction to danger.

Disorder is a clinical word that means your symptoms are getting in the way of your walking, talking everyday life - that's all.

That is one of the biggest reasons the PTSD rumor mill is so powerful. If you aren't able to access the information, you need in a format that makes sense, the only thing you are left with is hearsay.

Rumors and untruths will mess with your head and keep you from getting the treatment you deserve, so we're going to start off by dispelling a few right off the bat.

Why? Because "knowing is half the battle!"

We compiled this list of untruths: (1) from folks with PTSD, and (2) from actual masters and doctoral level clinicians whose job is to treat PTSD. So, if you heard one of these and believed it was true, you're in good company.

RUMOR 1

"PTSD Has No Treatment."

Add to this: "I'll always have PTSD," "I'll never get better," and "The symptoms may go away, but the PTSD will always be there." These are powerful beliefs so widely held that many folks give up before getting started.

FACT: There are three Evidence-Based Treatments (EBTs) for PTSD that have been given the stamp of approval by the Department of Veterans Affairs (VA). While PTSD is not exclusive to Service Members (we'll get to that in a minute), the VA puts a ton of money into research, and their stamp of approval means that these EBTs are widely available:

- Prolonged Exposure Therapy
- Cognitive Processing Therapy
- Eye-Movement Desensitization and Reprocessing Therapy

Tons of money has been thrown at PTSD research, and it's paying off in spades.

All three of the above mentioned EBTs have been proven to work for most people (we will take a deep dive into each of them in a later chapter).

Using an EBT for PTSD is important because EBTs are based on peer-reviewed scientific evidence. Researchers conduct rigorous studies using scientific methods, document their research in peer-reviewed scientific journals, and then other researchers conduct additional scientific studies to see if the treatment is, in fact, successful. It's a lot like how drugs are tested by the FDA - double-blind randomized trials over a long period of time with lots of scrutiny.

> Evidence-based treatment (EBT) is backed by scientific evidence. Studies have been conducted and extensive research has been documented on the particular treatment.
>
> It has proven to be successful.

When a therapy method is recognized as an EBT, it's a big deal.

There are folks who are labeled as "treatment-resistant," meaning that these three types of EBTs haven't worked for them, but researchers have found alternative treatments for them, like the use of Ketamine, MDMA-assisted psychotherapy, and faith-based treatments.

THE BOTTOM LINE

PTSD is treatable. EBTs work most of the time for most people. It doesn't matter how you feel; that's science. But hear this: nothing and no one can convince you something is true if you strongly believe it is not. That's science, too.

3

RUMOR 2

PTSD is only for Military Service Members or "I don't 'deserve' to have PTSD."

Many civilians believe that only military members can have PTSD. Within the military, many Service Members believe that only folks who engaged in active combat can have PTSD. Let's start by making this crystal clear:

**PTSD Can Develop In Anyone
Who Experiences Trauma.**

Anyone who has experienced, or continues to experience, trauma is at risk of developing PTSD. Period!

Continuing with that theme, we also need to clarify another point.

PTSD is not reserved only for those who have "earned it."

It's not a merit badge. It's not a punch card. No one wants to develop PTSD. It is a serious condition brought about as the result of dealing with some pretty awful crap.

Some clients make statements like, "I don't deserve to have PTSD. Other people have been through worse."

Let's have some real talk: No one deserves to have the flu. But flu doesn't care about that. No one deserves to have malaria or HIV or schizophrenia, but we don't get a choice. PTSD is same-same.

> **Truth Bomb**
>
> PTSD is something that happens *to you*,
> not something that is wrong *with you*.

Adding to that point, we need to understand that trauma comparison is not a valid gauge of individual experience. No two people will experience the same stressful or traumatic situation in the same way. What may traumatize one person may not feel that bad to another. Our experiences and our ability to cope are as individual as we are, so trying to compare traumas is like comparing apples to sports cars.

One of the EBTs for PTSD that focuses on "stuck points," or belief systems that keep us from getting better is **Cognitive Processing Therapy (CPT)**.

While working with individual clients and groups doing CPT, many variations of, "I don't deserve to have PTSD," come up, such as:

- I don't deserve to have PTSD because I froze/didn't fight back.
- I don't deserve to have PTSD because I was a child when my trauma happened.
- I don't deserve PTSD because I could have done something to prevent/stop it.

> **THE BOTTOM LINE**
>
> **No one deserves to have PTSD,** and we absolutely can come back from this.

RUMOR 3

People who develop PTSD are "not resilient" or "damaged goods."

This is the idea that someone "gets" PTSD because they are not resilient enough, or because they already experienced trauma, addiction, etc. and are "damaged goods." This rumor equates PTSD to the flu and opines that PTSD attacks those with compromised mental immune systems.

It is fantasy to believe that a happy childhood will inoculate us from future trauma. It won't! There is no quick "bounce back" for rape, war, or a serious accident, and we would appreciate it if people would stop pretending there was. Moreover, this rumor can have unintended consequences:

> Trauma is an individual experience. What makes something traumatic for one person may not be traumatic for another, depending on their relative ability to deal with it.

If people in need of help feel they will be labeled as "weak" or "damaged," then they will be less likely to seek the help they need.

Not seeking help can have disastrous effects. The following statistics are based on the U.S. population:[1] [2]

- About 6 out of every 100 people (or 6% of the population) will develop PTSD at some point during their life.
- About 8 of every 100 women (or 8%) develop PTSD sometime in their lives compared with about 4 of every 100 men (or 4%).

- Among people who have had a diagnosis of PTSD in their lifetime, approximately 27% have also attempted suicide.
- Women with Post-Traumatic Stress Disorder (PTSD) are nearly seven times more likely than other women to die by suicide .
- The average time between PTSD diagnosis and suicide was less than two and a half years.

THE BOTTOM LINE
PTSD symptoms are hard enough without blaming a survivor; this is cruel and unnecessary.

RUMOR 4

People who have a history of trauma cannot be high-functioning members of society.

When we define trauma and what someone with a trauma history looks like, we often miss out on seeing the truth of their personal history. We expect to see someone showing some form of self-destructive behavior in an attempt to self-sooth. But that is not always the case.

Trauma is often thought of as an isolated event: a car crash, Sexual Assault, or maybe something that happened during military service. While singular events can be traumatic, we're ignoring a whole host of ongoing situations and relational traumas a person can experience.

When a person is exposed to ongoing trauma, their mind tries to adapt. It's the brain's job to keep us alive, so in situations where we cannot escape our trauma, the brain switches from fight, flight, or freeze to a more adaptive tend-and-befriend mode (also known as fawning), allowing us to remain as safe as possible in the ongoing traumatic situation.

> We will cover many of the ongoing situations and relational traumas in Chapter 3.

In short, we develop coping mechanisms to keep everything peaceful. And, as long as things are relatively calm in our lives, we appear "normal."

In some cases, our focus is shifted outward, toward the things we can control: grades, promotions, seeking independence, and financial security. Many trauma survivors become fiercely independent because the betrayal they experienced left them knowing the only person they could rely on was themselves. (e.g. a former child of abusive or neglectful parents). To a spectator, these individuals seem like they have it all together. They couldn't possibly be struggling with PTSD, right?

Wrong.

If someone has to lean on self-sufficiency for survival, it is likely that by the time they desperately need help, they have perfected their mask of indifference and fortified their emotional barriers to the point that they have become reflexes. No longer aware of the walls they throw up, these people can be very difficult to diagnose.

Either way the pendulum swings, self-destructive or super high-functioning, the person who has experienced trauma (singular or ongoing) is attempting to compensate for it. And that may work for them for many years, until it doesn't.

THE BOTTOM LINE

Being outwardly high-functioning and needing trauma recovery work are not mutually exclusive. Just because someone appears to be high functioning, it doesn't mean they don't suffer.

Now that we know what PTSD is not, let's get down to brass tacks. Read on.

---

[1] National Center for PTSD https://www.ptsd.va.gov/understand/common/common_adults.asp

[2] Journal of Affective Disorders Volume 279, 15 January 2021, Pages 609-616 https://www.sciencedirect.com/science/article/pii/S0165032720328536

CHAPTER 2 WHAT IS PTSD?

Post-Traumatic Stress Disorder is the result of exposure to trauma, where the symptoms of that trauma persist or get worse in the weeks and months after the traumatic event.

Not everyone who is exposed to trauma or traumatic events will develop symptoms of PTSD, but many will.

Common symptoms of PTSD include:

- Intrusive thoughts
- Avoiding reminders of the trauma
- Flashbacks
- Startling easily
- Hypervigilance
- Anxiety
- Irritability
- Self-destructive behavior
- Loss of interest in activities
- Emotional detachment
- An increased risk for suicide[3].

That is the simple explanation for a complicated disorder. We've got a lot to cover as we take a deep dive into PTSD. For now, you need to know that exposure to trauma is the root cause. Understanding is the first step in recovery.

FACT: There is only one way to get an official PTSD diagnosis, and that is with a licensed clinician who knows their DSM-5.

HOW IS TRAUMA DEFINED IN THE DSM-5?

The *Diagnostic and Statistical Manual, Version Five (or Version Five Text Revision)*, should be on our therapist's bookshelf with the title *DSM-5 / DSM-5-TR* on the spine.

The version five came out in 2013, and this is important for us to know in case we got a diagnosis before 2013. **The clinical definition of PTSD changed *significantly* from version four to version five.** If you see the gray DSM-IV or DSM-IV TR on your therapist's shelf: RUN.

> The DSM-5 is the authoritative guide to the diagnosis of all mental disorders. It contains descriptions, symptoms, and criteria for diagnosis.

We have to have a no-kidding, sit-down with a mental health professional. It takes time and effort. We have to choose to be radically authentic with the clinician, and the clinician has to know their DSM-5. Hence, there are *a lot* of misdiagnoses out there.

The DSM is written by clinicians for clinicians. It has a lot of jargon and can be hard to understand.

To explain the facts of PTSD, we're going straight to the DSM-5 and providing a clinician-to-English translation.

When you discuss your PTSD with others, we want you to sound smart so that you can get the treatment you deserve and get your life back.

11

What Makes an Event Traumatic?

- It involves a threat—real or perceived—to one's physical or emotional well-being (Standard definition of trauma).

- It is overwhelming (Traumatic Stress).

- It results in intense feelings of fear and lack of control (Traumatic Stress).

- It leaves a feeling of helplessness (Traumatic Stress).

- It alters a person's perception of the world, themselves, and others (Moral Injury & Institutional Betrayal are big here).

Traumatic Stress is the stress response to a traumatic event. Traumatic Stress falls into a few categories. Many of us, especially those reading this book, have probably experienced a traumatic event or have dealt with Traumatic Stress in more than one form. So, let's break this down:

- **Acute Trauma**

  This is exposure to a single traumatic event.

- **Chronic Trauma**

  This is ongoing or prolonged exposure to Traumatic Stress or traumatic events.

- **Complex Trauma**

  This is exposure to multiple forms of trauma or traumatic events.

The current edition of the DSM-5 defines trauma as actual or threatened exposure to death, serious injury, or sexual violence.

Now that we know what exposure means, we need to understand how it applies, because that's where the expanded definition really helps us.

What this broader definition does is compensate for the fact that human physiology does not differentiate between implied or physical harm.

THE BOTTOM LINE

If you feel threatened, have been threatened, or are close to someone who has been threatened by physical harm or death, you can be traumatized by it.

And that's a big thing. Let's say that a little louder for the people in the back.

You Don't Need Physical Scars to Have Trauma.

Understanding that simple statement opens the door to exploring the different ways we are exposed to and deal with trauma in our lives. That leads to less stigma about trauma and better diagnosis and treatment options for those affected by it.

Since this book is geared toward women, before we get too far into the weeds, we have to discuss the elephant in the room.

THE GENDER DIFFERENCE WITH PTSD

While PTSD can happen to anyone, statistics show that there is a significant gender difference in the prevalence of PTSD. According to the National Center for PTSD[4], around 10% of women have PTSD sometime in their lives compared to 4% of men.

Approximately one half (50%) of all individuals will be exposed to at least one traumatic event in their lifetime.

> Women are twice as likely to develop PTSD, experience a longer duration of posttraumatic symptoms, and display more sensitivity to stimuli that remind them of the trauma.

The types of trauma might point to possible causes for the disparity.

Men are more likely to encounter traumas such as physical assault, accidents, disaster, combat, or to see death and injury. Women, on the other hand, are more prone to experience Sexual Assault, Emotional Abuse, and forced conformity to traditional gender roles (others controlling the power in social and relationship issues).

Numbers from the National Sexual Violence Resource Center[5] show that 91% of Sexual Assault survivors who come forward are women. Moreover, 20% of women will be sexually assaulted at some point in their lives. One study[6] found the effects of Sexual Assault are so damaging that 94% of women survivors experienced PTSD symptoms within the first two weeks following the incident.

The difference in coping strategies between men and women also plays a role in susceptibility to PTSD.

Men and women cope with stress differently.

Studies have found that men typically respond to stressful or threatening situations with "fight or flight" (and sometimes freeze). Women, however, are more likely to respond with "tend-and-befriend[7]."

TENDING involves taking care of people.

BEFRIENDING is the process of reaching out to people to create a network of support.

In simple terms, women are wired toward protecting, calming, and befriending in stressful situations as a method of diffusing rather than reacting by fight, flight, or freeze. This biological-behavioral response is at the core of our maternal instinct and stems from primitive reactions to threats, including predators, assaults, natural disasters, and any other threats to self and offspring.

To paraphrase a study by Doctor Shelley Taylor, et al., 2000[8]; if we consider a situation where a mother and her child are in danger; fighting and running is not a viable option. The mother cannot fight and ensure the safety of her child at the same time. She also cannot run away at top speed while dragging or carrying a child. In this case, they are both at higher risk of danger. However, by seeking help, the mother and child have a better chance of survival.

Safety in numbers. We all know this phrase. But, more than that, it is believed to be ingrained in our chemical response to stress. This instinct has been passed down, through the principle of natural selection, through subsequent generations.

A woman's "tend-and-befriend" instincts can create a reliance on the support of others during stressful or threatening situations.

In this case, it may make them more vulnerable to experiencing PTSD symptoms, especially if they feel rejected, abandoned, or isolated from their support network.

C-PTSD

While we are talking about PTSD, we also need to address Complex PTSD (C-PTSD). The two are similar in their root causes, with the C- distinction reflecting the complexity of issues that develop due to the repetitive nature of the trauma experienced over a long period of time.

> The distinction between PTSD and C-PTSD is important because many of the traumas we will outline in this book are ones that happen over long periods of time, and that alters the presentation and recovery treatments needed to heal.

The current edition of the *Diagnostic and Statistical Manual of Mental Disorders* (DSM-5) does not currently separate PTSD from C-PTSD, however, the World Health Organization (WHO) does include C-PTSD as its own separate diagnosis (6B41) in the 11th revision of the *International Statistical Classification of Diseases and Related Health Problems* (ICD-11).[9]

Because the diagnosis of C-PTSD is not included in the DSM-5 and the cluster of symptoms that present with this distinctive diagnosis often overlaps with other mood disorders, it can be difficult for clinicians to identify.

Many individuals who should be diagnosed with C-PTSD downplay their trauma and have developed unique coping mechanisms, which, more often than not, are failing by the time they are seeking help.

This makes them appear as high-functioning people, further confusing the diagnosis.

SYMPTOMS OF COMPLEX PTSD

C-PTSD has many of the same symptoms as PTSD, including intrusive memories or flashbacks, depression, anxiety, avoidance, and changes in personality. However, people with C-PTSD also experience:

- **Loss of Systems of Meaning**

  Losing core values, religion, beliefs, or faith can cause a sense of hopelessness and despair.

- **Negative Self-Perception**

  Experiencing helplessness, shame, guilt, and self-loathing, while often expressing feelings of inadequacy or being different from others.

- **Obsession with the Perpetrator of Trauma**

  And frequently changing perceptions of that perpetrator.

  A sexual abuse survivor, for example, might go back and forth between viewing the abuser as evil and loving, and might continue an unhealthy relationship with that person. Or they may become obsessed with ideas of getting revenge on the perpetrator of their trauma.

- **Changes in Consciousness**

  A person may have periods of amnesia (forgetting) or dissociation, making them feel detached from themselves or their surroundings.

- **Emotional Dysregulation**

  Difficulty in Controlling Emotions and/or Emotional flashbacks[10]

  Rather than intrusively remembering the traumatic event, a person with C-PTSD might instead become emotionally overwhelmed during periods of stress causing them to re-experience the emotions they felt during their trauma. This happens without recalling or thinking about the traumatic event. (e.g. it can manifest in the person breaking down and crying over a minor disagreement that wouldn't warrant such a strong emotional response.)

This distinction between PTSD and C-PTSD is important because many of the traumas we will outline in this book are ones that happen over long periods of time, and this extended duration of traumatic experiences often necessitates an altered and longer approach to treatment.

This extended treatment often includes cognitive processing of the trauma, emotional regulation skill building to overcome learned behaviors and habits that formed during the duration of the trauma, and a somatic level of work to help retrain the nervous system to function and respond appropriately instead of defaulting to stress responses.

This is especially important if the trauma experienced began during childhood.

---

[3] Karolina Krysinska & David Lester (2010) Post-Traumatic Stress Disorder and Suicide Risk: A Systematic Review, Archives of Suicide Research, 14:1, 1-23, DOI: 10.1080/13811110903478997

https://www.tandfonline.com/doi/abs/10.1080/13811109034789
97

[4] National Center for PTSD. How Common is PTSD in Women?
https://www.ptsd.va.gov/understand/common/common_women.asp

[5] National Sexual Violence Resource Center
https://www.nsvrc.org/sites/default/files/publications_nsvrc_fact-sheet_media-packet_statistics-about-sexual-violence_0.pdf

[6] Dworkin, Emily R., Anna E. Jaffe, Michele Bedard-Gilligan, and Skye Fitzpatrick. "PTSD in the Year Following Sexual Assault: A Meta-Analysis of Prospective Studies." Trauma, Violence, & Abuse, (July 2021).
https://doi.org/10.1177/15248380211032213.

[7] The tend-and-befriend theoretical model was originally developed by Dr. Shelley E. Taylor and her research team at the University of California, Los Angeles and first described in a Psychological Review article published in the year 2000. Biobehavioral Responses to Stress in Females:Tend-and-Befriend, Not Fight-or-Flight Shelley E. Taylor, Laura Cousino Klein, Brian P. Lewis, Tara L. Gruenewald, Regan A. R. Gurung, and John A. Updegraff. University of California, Los Angeles
https://scholar.harvard.edu/marianabockarova/files/tend-and-be-friend.pdf

[8] Biobehavioral Responses to Stress in Females:Tend-and-Befriend, Not Fight-or-Flight Shelley E. Taylor, Laura Cousino Klein, Brian P. Lewis, Tara L. Gruenewald, Regan A. R. Gurung, and John A. Updegraff. University of California, Los Angeles
https://scholar.harvard.edu/marianabockarova/files/tend-and-be-friend.pdf

[9] 6B41-Complex post-traumatic stress disorder
https://icd.who.int/browse11/l-m/en#/http://id.who.int/icd/entity/585833559

[10] Emotional Flashback Management in the Treatment of Complex PTSD https://www.psychotherapy.net/article/complex-ptsd

CHAPTER 3 TYPES OF TRAUMA

Before we dive into the technical parts of the DSM-5 and how it is used to diagnose and guide treatment for PTSD, we need to break down the various forms of trauma that are common exposure points, especially for women.

See how many you recognize:

- Childhood Trauma
- Abuse, Neglect, or Abandonment occurring in childhood (before 18 years of age)
- Emotional Abuse
- Sexual Assault or Domestic Violence
- Institutional Betrayal
- Moral Injury
- Medical Trauma
- Work Related Trauma
- Overwhelming Emotional Strain

We're going to dive a little deeper here and look at each of those points. One thing you'll notice is how many of the above-mentioned traumas overlap.

Remember this statistic?

Approximately one half (50%) of all individuals will be exposed to at least one traumatic event in their lifetime. And women are twice as likely to develop PTSD.

A quick note before we go into these individual topics:

The traumas we are about to go over may feel triggering, especially if you have or are currently experiencing them.

We will also be sharing true stories from survivors who have been through these same traumatic events.

The goal of this book is to help the healing process, show you that you are not alone, and empower you to take back your life, and guide you toward recovering your mental health.

For that reason, we will not use the word victim.

YOU ARE A SURVIVOR.

CHILDHOOD TRAUMA

Childhood Trauma is strongly associated with developing mental health problems. We mentioned earlier that C-PTSD was also linked to ongoing and relational trauma, especially when the trauma begins during a person's youth. We expect that many of the adults reading this book will find the experiences we're about to cover of particular interest.

Adverse Childhood Experiences (ACEs) [11]is the term used to describe the types of abuse, neglect, or other potentially traumatic experiences that can happen to a person under the age of 18.

Trauma can come from a variety of experiences. Common examples of trauma that children and adolescents can experience include things like:

- Sexual Abuse / Rape
- Neglect
- Emotional Abuse / Narcissistic Parent
- School Violence / Bullying
- Natural Disasters
- Military-Family Related Stressors
- Sudden or Violent Loss of a Loved One
- Serious Accidents
- Life-Threatening Illnesses

NPR has a basic Adverse Childhood Experiences quiz you can take as a sample self-assessment to get started on your healing journey[12]. *The link will be in the resources section of this book.*

It is important to recognize that upsetting experiences are not always traumatic.

Divorce, for example, is an upsetting experience for children. It can create a feeling of abandonment or parental loss in a child, but the divorce alone is not necessarily traumatizing. How the parents handle the divorce, however, can be. If one parent attempts to use the child as a pawn with the other parent, that can create a traumatic situation for the child. Situational context is important.

In most cases of abuse, it is the caregiver who is identified as the perpetrator—someone the child knows and relies on for care: a parent, teacher, religious leader, coach, or family physician.

This includes direct abuse and/or negligence in reporting abuse involving a child and caregiver. Betrayal Blindness[13] is a term used to describe an unwillingness to recognize abuse that is ongoing.

We should also note that many children who are exposed to potentially traumatic events may experience initial distress, but it is short-lived. In the case of PTSD, it is the duration of symptoms that categorize the disorder. That is not to downplay the seriousness of trauma. Again, context is important.

Statistically, between 3-15% of girls and 1-6% of boys develop PTSD following a traumatic event. [14]

Children who don't develop PTSD may still exhibit emotional and behavioral issues following a traumatic experience:

- Anger Issues
- Attention Problems
- Changes in Appetite

- Development of New/Irrational Fears
- Increased Thoughts About Death or Safety
- Irritability
- Loss of Interest in Normal Activities/School
- Problems Sleeping

Behavioral changes in the child can also exacerbate the problem of abuse, especially when physical or mental abuse was the initial trauma that was experienced by the child.

Let's look at physically abusive caregivers as the cause of trauma, for an example. Let's say the child begins to show signs of anger issues and attention problems following an instance of abuse. They lose the interest and or desire to attend school or other activities. This can twist into a cycle of abuse if the child is seen as delinquent and needing to be punished for their unwillingness to do what is expected of them. This can lead the abusive caregiver to continue physically punishing the child in an effort to force them to correct their behavior.

A child's relationship with their caregiver—parents, family, coaches, teachers, etc.—is vital to their emotional and physical health. When a child experiences a trauma related to that caregiver, it can create a sense of distrust, both in their caregiver and in their environment. They may begin to view the world as a scary place and all adults as potentially dangerous.

This affects their ability to form healthy relationships as they continue to grow, causing problems with romantic relationships, peer relationships, and any other attachment-based relationships.

There is also a concept called Intergenerational Trauma[15]

that speaks to the passing down of trauma through generations. Exposure to extremely adverse events in childhood can affect an individual so much that their offspring are affected by their parents' post-traumatic state. While this was initially identified among children of Holocaust survivors, it can apply to child abuse survivors, too. [16]

PERSONAL EXPERIENCE

Part of me doesn't feel like blaming my mother for how horrible she was to me is justified. She didn't have it easy growing up. My grandmother was textbook narcissist. My mother was the scapegoat, while her brother was the golden child.

She'd often tell me how she had to hide bruises or black eyes. The old "Walked into a door" excuse was enough back then to avoid any caring people from looking into her home life.

When I think of how she must have felt growing up in a home where she believed she was unloved or not good enough, it makes sense that she threw herself into her schoolwork.

She wasn't a straight-A student because she loved school or learning. It was her refuge. At some point, she must have thought the good grades would earn her some love, but from what she told me, that wasn't the case.

When she turned eighteen, my mother found the military. An escape that took her far away from her family.

If I stopped there, you might think this was a happy ending. But the reality is, that was just the beginning of my story.

Fast forward ten years, and I found myself cornered in the bathroom as my mother raged at me. What started as a pleasant afternoon visiting with my grandmother went completely sideways the moment I returned home.

Once again, I found myself caught in the middle of their ongoing generational struggle.

A Struggle I worry I will be doomed to repeat, seeing as all the women in my family apparently hate each other.

Things had been tense since my grandmother moved to town. Three houses down from ours, on the same street, to be exact.

The adults never clued me in to their tension, not that I should have expected it to, seeing as I was still very much a child. But, being a child, you pick up on things. Subtle clues, snippets of conversation. The tension was there, and it was thick.

But as my mother slowly backed me down the hall and into the bathroom, demanding I tell her everything my grandmother had said, my ten-year-old brain couldn't work fast enough to appease her.

Was I supposed to make something up? That's what my mother wanted. Some evidence that my grandmother was badmouthing her. That would give her a reason to sever any remaining ties to her family, and maybe demand she move away.

But my grandmother was smarter than that. She wouldn't dare say something negative to me about my mother. If grandma wanted to hurt my mom, she'd do it herself.

At that moment, however, I was the one in danger of being hurt.

Thankfully, I did not grow up in the don't-ask-don't-tell era of child abuse. If I showed up at school with a black eye, someone was bound to ask questions. My mother knew that. She wouldn't strike me anywhere that would leave evidence. Her attacks would come in the form of manipulation and emotional abuse.

So unless I wanted to be ridiculed for being a simpering, stupid, worthless, baby, I had to say something to calm her down and appease her rage.

I've always worried that the narcissist gene (I know that's not a real thing) that came from my grandmother and clearly transferred to my mother might be passed down to me at some point.

The constant fear that I am a terrible mother has led me, more often than I would like to admit, to question if I'm too harsh or too much of a doormat with my kids. I'm constantly second-guessing my mothering skills and praying that I don't repeat the same mistakes or pass the narcissistic gene down to my three little ones.

Experiencing child mistreatment can affect future parenting in nuanced ways.

Because of the consequences of their own mistreatment, parents with a history of abuse and neglect often have less capability to cope with the challenges of raising children.

They may have untreated mental health issues impairing their judgement. They may be dealing with unresolved anxiety, depression, or have issues with attachment-based relationships. They also lack a good example of what good caregiving practices look like and often revert to the parenting practices they experienced as a guideline when raising their own children. This can lead to a continuing cycle of childhood mistreatment.[17]

BULLYING

Bullying, also known as peer victimization, is an Adverse Childhood Experience (ACE).

ACEs are potentially traumatic events that can have negative, lasting effects on a person's development, the way they interact with others, and how they perform in school.

It is aggressive behavior, often seen among school-aged children (but can also happen during adulthood), that involves inflicting of social, emotional, physical, and/or psychological harm to someone who often is perceived as being less powerful.

There are three types of bullying:

VERBAL BULLYING INCLUDES:

- Teasing
- Name-calling
- Inappropriate sexual comments
- Taunting
- Threatening to cause harm

SOCIAL BULLYING involves hurting someone's reputation or relationships and includes in person and online interactions:

- Leaving someone out on purpose
- Telling other children not to be friends with someone
- Spreading rumors about someone
- Embarrassing someone in public
- Sharing personal or private information about someone

PHYSICAL BULLYING involves hurting a person or their possessions:

- Hitting/kicking/pinching
- Spitting
- Tripping/pushing

- Taking or breaking someone's things
- Making mean or rude hand gestures

Bullying can occur during or after school hours. While most reported bullying happens in the school building, a significant percentage also happens in places like the playground or the school bus.

It can also happen travelling to or from school, in the child's neighborhood, or on the Internet.

CYBERBULLYING, which is a modern form of social bullying, has introduced another level of unique concerns which have significant impacts on children:

The current social media environment increases the spread of hurtful information or harassment beyond the local community setting.

- Digital devices offer an ability to immediately and continuously communicate making it difficult for children to find relief from online harassment.
- Most information communicated electronically is permanent and public, if not reported and removed.
- A negative online reputation can impact college admissions, employment, and other areas of life.
- Teachers and parents may not overhear or see cyberbullying taking place, making it harder to recognize unless reported.

Research shows that females use more relational aggression, while males engage in physical bullying[18].

Gender stereotypes play a role in bullying because they directly influence the socialization of young children into gender roles.

Males are socialized to be strong and independent, while females are socialized to be understanding and sensitive. We're not saying that females won't be physically aggressive or boys won't exclude others, but the statistics seem to follow the gender trends.

The 2019 School Crime Supplement (SBS) to the National Crime Victimization Survey (National Center for Education Statistics and Bureau of Justice) shows that, nationwide, about 22% of students ages 12–18 experienced bullying[19].

The 2019 Youth Risk Behavior Surveillance System (YRBS) shows that, nationwide, 19.5% of students in grades 9–12 report being bullied on school property in the 12 months preceding the survey[20].

Females tend to bully other people indirectly or by using social or relational aggression. This type of bullying includes verbal assaults, ostracizing, spreading rumors, and gossiping. One of the biggest problems with this type of bullying is the ability to disguise their actions through passive-aggressive behavior, which makes this type of bullying more difficult to spot.

> Because of the socially-geared nature of the female gender, or those identifying as female, many young girls engage in bullying because of peer pressure and the desire to be part of the popular group.

In general, girls do not bully on their own, they tend to belong to a group, where everyone that follows shares in the behavior. Remember *Mean Girls*[21], the 2004 American teen comedy film directed by Mark Waters and written by Tina Fey? That's exactly the type of clique-style bullying we're talking about here.

Girls may also engage in relational aggression as a result of jealousy, low self-esteem, boredom, or learned behavior from others.

Females also experience sexual bullying more than males[22]. This includes spreading rumors of sexual activity and direct sexual harassment.

SEXTING—sending or receiving sexually explicit messages or images between electronic devices—is becoming increasingly common.

Research shows that among kids between the ages of 11 and 17, 15% of them sent sexts and 27% received sexts; the prevalence of the behavior increases as adolescents age[23].

When sexts are sent without consent, such as when private nude photos or videos of an individual are widely shared among a peer group, it can lead to sexual bullying and even Sexual Assault.

The 2019 Youth Risk Behavior Surveillance System CDC data mentioned above also includes data on sexual orientation and gender identity, giving additional depth via gender and non-binary statistics.

The Human Rights Campaign tabulated the results from the 2019 Youth Risk Behavior Surveillance System CDC data. Results revealed that statistically, lesbian, gay, bisexual, transgender, queer, intersex, non-binary or otherwise gender non-conforming (LGBTQI+) youth and those perceived as LGBTQI+ are at an increased risk of being bullied[24].

- 29% of transgender youth have been threatened or injured with a weapon on school property, compared to 7% of cisgender youth.

31

- 16% of gay and lesbian youth and 11% of bisexual youth have been threatened or injured with a weapon on school property, compared to 7% of straight youth.
- 43% of transgender youth have been bullied on school property, compared to 18% of cisgender youth.
- 29% of gay or lesbian youth and 31% of bisexual youth have been bullied on school property, compared to 17% of straight youth.

In other words, children that exist outside of cisgender identities tend to be targeted more often by bullies.

Regardless of the nationwide numbers, the impact of being exposed to this specific type of trauma comes with potential long-lasting consequences. Those who have been on the receiving end of bullying often develop hyperarousal symptoms, feeling like they could be attacked or criticized at any time. Even if the abuse stops, they may live in anticipation and fear, waiting for the next incident to occur. This combination of restless feelings may lead to performance decline, isolation behaviors, and low self-esteem.

A 2012 study[25] found that for all students who experienced bullying, 27.6% of boys and 40.5% of girls had PTSD scores within the clinical range.

Symptoms were even worse for those students who both bullied others and had been the targets of bullying themselves.

Children who have experienced trauma are more likely to be bullied and to engage in bullying behavior.

Children who experience trauma may develop social or interpersonal difficulties, making them more likely to become targets of bullying.

Studies of Adverse Childhood Experiences[26], or ACEs, have found that children who report more ACEs are also more likely to exhibit bullying behavior.

Bullying isn't just traumatic in childhood, though. Research shows bullying and harassment can cause adult symptoms of PTSD[27], [28]. In fact, one study examining mental health in college students found experiencing bullying to be the strongest predictor of developing PTSD symptoms.

Another literature review examining 29 relevant studies on bullying and harassment found that 57% of victims scored above the threshold for PTSD symptoms[29].

THE BOTTOM LINE

Being bullied, in any form, can severely affect a child's self-image, social interactions, or school performance, and can lead to mental health problems.

TOXIC SHAME

In the 1960s, psychologist Silvan Tomkins[30] coined the term "toxic shame" to refer to a deep and debilitating pathology that results from traumatic experiences of being repeatedly humiliated, rejected, despised, and treated as worthless.

In 1988, counselor, speaker, and author John Bradshaw brought Toxic Shame into public awareness in his self-help book, *Healing The Shame That Binds You.*[31]

Shame is a feeling of diminished self-worth that is not related to any particular action.

Guilt is a negative feeling related to a particular action.

A personal favorite of mine, Brené Brown[32], who has spent decades studying courage, vulnerability, shame, and empathy, describes shame as,

"The intensely painful feeling or experience of believing that we are flawed and therefore unworthy of love and belonging — something we've experienced, done, or failed to do makes us unworthy of connection."

Toxic Shame has its roots in criticism. Most criticism is intended to correct a behavior, however, when the focus of that criticism is that *you*, rather than *your behavior choices*, are the problem, the seed of shame is planted.

The aggressor in this situation is not trying to correct choices.

They are focusing their negativity on the survivor, selecting things that are out of the survivor's control to use for a personal attack.

Toxic Shame is prevalent in family situations. Parents who may have endured treatment like this when they were children often replicate the behavior with their own children.

It is not always easy to see the intent of criticism when it is delivered, and that is why this cycle of shame can go unnoticed, becoming toxic.

PERSONAL EXPERIENCE

School years were the hardest for me. I might have been a slow reader with more than a touch of undiagnosed ADHD, but I wasn't stupid, despite the numerous insinuating messages I got during my formative years. Grades were all that mattered, though, and report cards were the bane of my existence. I dreaded bringing them home. Without fail, there would always be one subject I was failing or close to failing. And that, simply wasn't allowed.

I can still remember the speech.

"When I was your age, I wouldn't dare bring home a report card with anything less than straight-A's. My mother would knock me into next Tuesday if she saw so much as a single B. But here you are, a failure. You didn't even get an A in one class. You know what happens to people who get grades like this? They end up flipping burgers for the rest of their lives. Is that what you want? You want to be a burger flipper? Because that is all you will ever amount to in this life."

There's nothing wrong with a career in the food industry. Whether it is flipping burgers or being a Michelin-rated chef. But that wasn't my mother's point. Her aim was simply to shame me into getting better grades. I know that now. But back then, it felt like she had already determined my worth. In her eyes, I was lacking.

I wanted to do better. I wanted to make her proud. And for one brief moment, I thought I had.

I made the A-B honor roll. It was a first for me, and I was certain she would be happy. But as I handed over the report card, awaiting my verbal gold star, her lips twisted into a scowl.

"Why are there so many B's?"

I was crushed. My achievement meant nothing, because it wasn't perfection.

While I'm sure she thought she was motivating me to aspire to be better, the message I got was, "Anything less than absolute perfection would doom me to a life of impoverished servitude, so I had better make peace with that."

At that point I no longer cared what grades I got. It was clear nothing I did would ever be good enough.

From that point on, I no longer cared about my grades. She could point out my stupidity all she wanted. By the time I was in middle school, I could recite the damn burger flipper speech. It had become little more than a cliché at that point. My goal was to get to eighteen and get the hell out of the house as fast as possible, so I did just enough to keep myself from being held back in school.

The moment I could escape, I did. But leaving home and becoming fully responsible came with its own set of problems, financial, and educational setbacks.

Even now, as I struggle against perfectionist tendencies and my own inner critic — while desperately trying to get my business off the ground so I can earn enough to feel secure — I can hear the echoes of her voice.

Did she curse me to a life of flipping burgers, or did I doom myself in spite of her? After attempting and subsequently dropping out of college because I couldn't juggle working full time while going to school, is that all I am truly qualified to do?

While it is more commonly seen in the parent/child relationship, Toxic Shame can show up in any close relationship with another person.

When shame is used intentionally, **it is Emotional Abuse**. It is done with the intent of keeping the survivor powerless and at the mercy of the abuser.

If the survivor's sense of personal value has been diminished by Toxic Shame, they feel worthless. And because they feel that they are worthless, they also do not feel they deserve the help they need.

Let's stop right here. Take a moment and read the following statement.

You are not worthless.
You deserve to feel comfortable in your own skin.
You deserve to heal.

Read it again. Keep reading that statement until you believe it, because, friend, you do deserve to heal. And until you believe it, you cannot begin to heal.

To get an idea of how shaming becomes toxic, let's look at a child wetting the bed. This is a common thing, both frustrating for the parent and child. No one likes to be woken up in the middle of the night in a puddle of their own creation.

The child will naturally go to the parent for help. No parent likes to be roused from sleep to clean up a mess, and, let's face it, we're certainly not at our best when this happens.

So let's try an example approach to this problem.

"Try to remember to go potty before bed next time. Let's get this cleaned up quickly so we can get back to bed."

A neutral response aimed at correcting the situation quickly. *Go potty before bed. Clean up the mess.*

"Again? Why can't you hold your damn bladder like your sister does? I am so sick of cleaning up your messes."

A direct criticism of the child for something they may not have control over. *It is common for children up to 9 years old to have occasional bed-wetting incidents.*

That second response is a direct critique of the child that diminishes their value by comparing them to a sibling who does not wet the bed.

Now, we're all human, and occasionally say things we don't mean. We're not implying that saying something like the above statement, one time, will create Toxic Shame.

In our example, **repeated exposure** to response two might lead the child to associate themselves with negative self-talk, such as, "I am a worthless bed wetter."

Common Negative Self-Talk Themes with Toxic Shame Include:

- I am a terrible person.
- I do not matter.
- I am unattractive.
- I am stupid.
- I should have never been born.
- I don't deserve love.
- I will never amount to anything.

THE BOTTOM LINE

Shame becomes toxic when there is repeated exposure to constant criticism—directed at the person rather than their actions—that results in a permanent state of negative self-talk.

THE NARCISSISTIC PARENT

Children of narcissistic parents are often subjected to years of emotional manipulation, neglect, and abuse which goes unnoticed by outsiders.

These children are often not even aware of the abuse they are experiencing until it manifests later in life as difficult to diagnose mental health issues.

But before we can understand how the narcissistic parent abuses their child, we must first understand what narcissism is and how the disorder presents.

Narcissistic Personality Disorder (NPD): a psychological personality disorder, defined by The DSM-5, characterized by an inflated sense of one's own importance, a deep need for excessive attention and admiration, troubled relationships, and a lack of empathy for others.

Because we're not diagnosing anyone in this book, we won't go into the lengthy definition of this disorder.

What we want to focus on, however, are the key traits, because they do an excellent job illustrating how this disorder applies to the abuse that narcissistic parents can cause their children.

Lack of Empathy

This is probably the single biggest defining trait of a narcissist. The inability to identify with and/or unwillingness to recognize the experiences and feelings of other people.

In other words. The narcissist neither cares nor wants to understand how other people feel.

Grandiose Sense of Self-Importance

These people exaggerate accomplishments, talents, connections, and experiences. *These do not have to be actual experiences.*

Grandiose people often have a preoccupation with fantasies of success, power, brilliance, beauty, or ideal love. They live in a fantasy world of their own creation. One where they are the center of attention and the most important person.

This belief they are unique and can only be understood by, or should associate with, other special or high-status people or institutions bleeds into their everyday interactions with the real world.

Need for Excessive Admiration

These people are often covering for some deep emotional wound, and in order to avoid the pain of it, they constantly need praise and approval to keep their spirits up. With this trait, the person with NPD will surround themselves with others who constantly boost their ego. They do not; however, reciprocate.

Sense of Entitlement

Living in a fantasy world of their own imagining, these people consider themselves to be special and act accordingly. They expect favorable treatment. Those who do not meet their expectations are treated with aggression and outrage.

Exploitative Behavior

The need for admiration, coupled with a sense of entitlement, and their inability to empathize with others, means the person with NPD will only surround themselves with people who do and say what they want. This becomes their standard. Their circle exists to serve them, and they do not think twice about using their people to get what they want.

Envious of Others

Narcissists feel threatened whenever they encounter someone who appears to have something they lack—confidence, popularity, better looks, or possess skills they do not. Their defense mechanism is contempt. They may patronize or dismiss the value of others whom they are secretly envious of. Or they attack with insults, bullying, or other forms of character assassination to neutralize the threat.

One more thing we have to touch on. This one is a big deal, especially for children who are exposed to it.

Narcissistic Rage.

This term was first coined by author Heinz Kohut[33] in 1972 to refer to the tendency for people with NPD to fly into a powerful outburst that can include anger, aggression, and violence, often with only the slightest provocation.

This rage is child-like in nature and goes straight from the feeling of stress to a full-blown explosive reaction[34]. Narcissists, as we've established, have little to no capability for empathy. Because of

> According to the DSM-5, "Vulnerability in self-esteem makes individuals with narcissistic personality disorder very sensitive to 'injury' from criticism or defeat. Although they may not show it outwardly, criticism may haunt these individuals and leave them feeling humiliated, degraded, hollow, and empty.

that, the narcissist rarely feels remorse after such an outburst—if anything, they will justify their actions as a protective response from the (perceived) hurt given to them that caused the outburst to begin with. They may react with disdain, rage, or defiant counterattack.[35]"

In short, Narcissists believe they are being attacked.

For those of you out there who remember the film, *Mommy Dearest,* which came out in 1981, you might have an idea where we are going with this. If not, we urge you to Google it. The "no more wire hangers," scene is priceless.

While it is a slight exaggeration, the movie is a harrowing look into what children growing up in a household with an NPD parent is like[36].

Now that we know the base traits, we can look at how having a narcissistic parent exposes the child to **long-term Emotional Abuse**, **neglect**, **and** in some cases **violence** (Our Big Three for Childhood Trauma).

Remember that those with NPD are highly sensitive, defensive, and lack empathy for other people, which extends to their children.

Common Characteristics of Narcissistic Parents:
- Focusing all the family's time and attention on themselves
- Not showing concern or compassion for their children or other family members
- Blaming others when things don't go according to plan (scapegoating their children)
- Not taking ownership of situations or acknowledging their wrongs
- Codependent or controlling with their children

- Ruling the household by domination, fear, manipulation
- Teasing, mocking, bullying, or Gaslighting (e.g. they publicly embarrass or shame) their children
- Love is (conditional) awarded or denied based on the behavior of the child

Narcissists come across as being very arrogant and over-confident people, but the reality is, they are insecure and need constant admiration and attention.

In public, they come across as social, charming, funny, and friendly, often appearing like the perfect parent. A narcissistic parent may be a class parent, PTO president, or soccer coach. But that involvement is self-serving. They do it for the attention and need to be involved in every aspect of their child's life.

They will seek attention by bragging about their special golden child's achievements. In other cases, they may use their child as the scapegoat, earning attention for how difficult their lives are because they try so hard with such a disobedient child to rear.

Golden Child vs. Scapegoat.

Golden Child: A golden child can't do anything wrong. They are the smartest and the best at everything they do. This is what the narcissistic parent believes and will enforce this belief in that child.

The golden child is the extension of the narcissistic parent. A narcissist considers themselves to be perfect, so the extension of themselves (the golden child) must be perfect, too.

Scapegoat: Everything the scapegoat does is wrong, not as good as it should be, and they always have to take the blame (even if they aren't the ones to blame). The scapegoat stands for everything that is not perfect in the family.

That child can't be good at anything, because he or she represents all that is wrong. A narcissist considers themselves to be perfect, so whenever things don't go well, it must be because of someone else.

> Being the Golden Child or the Scapegoat is more common in families with more than 1 child; however, in singleton households, an only child may act as both the golden child and the scapegoat, since the narcissistic parent needs to use them.

Children raised in narcissistic households run a greatest risk of estrangement (from parents or siblings) in their adult lives due to their parents demanding, highly critical, and shaming, according to Dr. Kylie Agllias, author of *Family Estrangement: A Matter of Perspective.*

Children in these families tend to shut down, numbing themselves to their emotions, which eventually limits all of their relationships.

At home is where the real narcissist comes out.

Their need to feel superior manifests in extreme levels of control over their children. The narcissistic mother or father must get what he or she wants.

Children growing up in a household with a narcissistic parent learn to fit into the molds that their parent creates for them. This can lead to anxiety for the child who must constantly push aside their own needs, wants, and desires in order to please the parent. Asserting their own feelings or thoughts can lead to problems with the parent that often include anger and punishment. Through this, the child learns that their feelings and thoughts are unimportant and will often stifle their own feelings in order to keep the peace at home.

Here are some telltale signs you may have a narcissistic parent:

- Constantly makes the conversation to be about themselves
- Brags about child's achievements to others, but rarely validates or acknowledges the child personally
- Blames others for any problems the child may have that stem from their behavior
- Is well-liked and important to others, but controlling and harsh when no one is looking
- Makes their child feel bad for not doing what they (the parent) want immediately
- Makes the child feel guilty by boasting about how much they (the parent) do for the child
- Harshly opinionated at home but puts up a front for people they dislike (two-faced)
- Ruthless and unforgiving, doing anything they can to be on top
- Makes their child feel anxious and often lowers their confidence (belittling)
- Is absent from child's important life events
- Forces athletics, clubs, or other extracurricular activities on their child, even if the child does not wish to participate
- Provides no emotional support or nurturing
- Uses children for personal gain
- Is bothered by child's need for attention

- Limits time with children unless it serves their (the parent's) own needs
- Displays erratic behaviors or sudden mood changes, especially anger (narcissistic rage)

Children of narcissists are typically discouraged from setting boundaries. A narcissist seems incapable of recognizing that other people have needs, so they will not respect the boundaries their child attempts to set. They freely intrude, stay enmeshed in their child's lives, and discourage their children's individuality. While they are intruding, a narcissistic parent will also make their child feel guilty for any boundary the child dares to set. Guilt and manipulation are common ways that your boundaries are breached, framed in such a way that the child's obedience is owed to the parent. This keeps the children easier to control.

As an adult, children of narcissistic parents have trouble expressing their thoughts, making decisions, or managing conflict. Feeling unheard and "invisible" may be a frequent experience.

Children of narcissists do not experience healthy communication. The narcissistic parent may make a habit of putting down their children, making sure the child knows who is superior and in control. They may make unfavorable comparisons, use subtle humiliations, and engage in unhealthy competition. These are all ways to invalidate the child and wear down self-esteem. It leaves the child starved for affection *and* subservient.

As an adult, children of narcissistic parents often have an ingrained response to fawn. Making themselves and their needs vanish so they can focus on keeping others happy. This survival strategy is actually a suppression of the fight-or-flight response.

Having been raised in a situation of constant verbal warfare, these survivors learned that placating avoided the worst of conflict. This behavior bleeds into their daily life, leaving them with low self-esteem and a people-pleasing personality that makes them vulnerable to being taken advantage of.

Children of narcissists experience manipulation and Gaslighting regularly. When provoked, narcissistic parents respond with mockery, humiliation, and threats of violence or neglect. If the child attempts to defend themselves, the narcissist will twist the situation around, and accuse the child of attacking them. Often narcissistic people will punish their children by mounting a smear campaign against them, badmouthing the child to others to gain sympathy while damaging their child's reputation. This effectively keeps the child quiet, frustrated, and prone to doing their parents' bidding for the sake of peace.

As an adult, children of narcissistic parents have experienced so many mind games, they are plagued with self-doubt and rarely trust their perceptions. Their lack of self-confidence leads to chronic difficulty in making decisions. And with no one to trust, having been alienated through the destruction of their reputation, many feel as if no one can understand or believe their story.

Children of narcissists are often the target of narcissistic rage. (outbursts which can include gaslighting, verbal abuse, threats of violence, or stonewalling). Narcissists are highly sensitive individuals that require a steady supply of positive attention. When they feel slighted, it triggers an angry and sometimes violent outburst. Because of the reactivity and intensity of the parent's emotional outbursts, children are left with little to no coping skills to learn how to regulate their own emotions.

As an adult, children of narcissistic parents may feel overwhelmed and uncomfortable, particularly when facing criticism, conflict, or disapproval.

Even after growing up in an environment filled with lies, manipulation, and abuse, it can be difficult for adult children of narcissistic parents to step away from caring for and loving their abusive parent. These people have been raised to serve in a family setting where love is conditional.

Untreated trauma can erode development, sense of safety, and trust. This stunts the child's sense of self as deserving of compassion, honesty, and respect, as well as their perception of the world as predictable, fair, and safe.

Prolonged exposure to trauma changes the way we develop, while our learned experiences influence our perception of the world and how we interact with the world and people as an adult.

This prevents them from developing and maintaining healthy and secure attachments leaving them urgently craving emotional intimacy, while simultaneously recoiling from any close relationships.

Lack of personal agency and connection to others leaves the child powerlessness, and in a constant state of self-doubt and shame.

Adults can suffer from PTSD or be prone to finding themselves in abusive relationships with narcissists, just like their parents. In some cases they may also turn into narcissistic adults, continuing the cycle.

Not all survivors of childhood mistreatment will repeat the behavior with their children, however, an estimated one-third of people who have been subjected to child abuse and neglect do continue the same abusive patterns with their children.

Breaking away from the cycle of abuse requires not only learning the difference between genuine love and narcissistic love, but it also requires the adult child of a narcissistic parent to come to terms with the fact that they've experienced years of Emotional Abuse and constant Gaslighting.

Many adult children find that the most healthy option for them is to sever the relationship altogether, but that only cuts off contact. It does not address the underlying damage that has been done. Unlike someone who has experienced a traumatic event in adulthood and developed symptoms of PTSD, complex trauma stemming from childhood has taken years to take root.

Therapy is essential to know the extent of the trauma and to work through the steps to heal from it. [37.]

THE BOTTOM LINE

Children, exposed to complex trauma, especially when originating from someone they know and trust, is a risk factor for nearly all behavioral health and substance use disorders. The impact of childhood trauma, whether single instances or long-term abuse carries impacts that can last well beyond childhood.

CHILDHOOD SEXUAL ABUSE

As defined by the 1999 WHO Consultation on Child Abuse Prevention:[38]

Child sexual abuse is the involvement of a child in sexual activity that he or she does not fully comprehend, is unable to give informed consent to, or for which the child is not developmentally prepared and cannot give consent, or that violates the laws or social taboos of society. Child sexual abuse is evidenced by this activity between a child and an adult or another child who, by age or development, is in a relationship of responsibility, trust, or power, the activity being intended to gratify or satisfy the needs of the other person.

This may include, but is not limited to:

- The inducement or coercion of a child to engage in any unlawful sexual activity
- The exploitative use of a child in prostitution or other unlawful sexual practices
- The exploitative use of children in pornographic performance and materials

This is one of the most stigmatized issues in society and is recognized as a violation of basic human rights and a serious public health concern. However, the prevalence of Childhood Sexual Abuse can be difficult to accurately measure since it is under-reported.

Even more unsettling are the numbers of Childhood Sexual Abuse Statistics:

- About 1 in 4 girls and 1 in 13 boys experience sexual abuse in childhood.
- 91% of Childhood Sexual Abuse is perpetrated by someone the child or child's family knows.
- Studies show that children between the ages of 7 and 13 are the most vulnerable to Childhood Sexual Abuse.

- Survivors of Childhood Sexual Assault have an increased likelihood of being assaulted again in adulthood.
- Females exposed to Child Sexual Abuse are at 2-13 times increased risk of sexual victimization in adulthood.
- Individuals who experienced Childhood Sexual Abuse are at twice the risk for non-sexual intimate partner violence. [39]

With Childhood Sexual Abuse, physical force or violence are rarely used. The perpetrator is typically known and is considered a trusted caregiver. The abuser will often take on a father figure, counselor, teacher, or older sibling-like role so they can gain close access to children.

The abuser is also likely to develop close relationships with the child's family to maintain consistent access to the child.

Abuse, in this case, happens slowly, usually over weeks-to-years, becoming more invasive with time. They may desensitize the child with harmless touching before violating them sexually. This slow adaptive strategy disarms the child, their family, or other caregivers. And it is extremely difficult to detect.

> This pattern of behavior is called grooming.

Incest or intra-familial abuse is another form of Childhood Sexual Abuse that accounts for about one third of all child sexual abuse cases. Many children remain with their abusers, especially when the abuse is happening within their family unit.

51

It's hard to estimate how many cases of child sexual abuse go undetected or are ignored via Betrayal Blindness (see Childhood Trauma).

Most cases that are reported are often delayed due to Child Sexual Abuse Accommodation Syndrome (CSAAS), a term coined by Roland Summit, MD in 1983.

CSAAS has roughly 5 parts:

- **Secrecy**—Children may fear the abuser's retribution, or they may have been promised something in return for keeping their mouth shut.

- **Helplessness**—Children are naturally in a helpless or subordinate state compared to adults. They may not feel they can fight back.

- **Entrapment and Accommodation**—Children feel trapped by the secrecy and ongoing nature of the abuse and become adapted to their situation.

- **Delayed Disclosure**—Children may be fearful of the outcome of revealing their abuse. They may downplay or sound unconvincing on the first attempt which can lead to the disclosure being ignored. That may lead the child to avoid coming forward again if they feel there will be no positive outcome.

- **Retraction**—When a disclosure is made by the child, they may be re-traumatized by revealing and experiencing the event, leading them to retract their statement. This is because the more they have to explain, the more they re-live the event's trauma.

Physical and behavioral changes are often the first signs that abuse is happening.

Physical:

- Sleep Disturbances
- Bedwetting
- Pain or Irritation in Genital/Anal Area
- Difficulty Walking or Sitting
- Difficultly Urinating
- Pregnancy
- Sexually Transmitted Disease
- Excessive Masturbation

Behavioral:

- Developmental Age-Inappropriate Sexual Play and/or Drawings
- A Sudden Aggression and/or Cruelty to Others and/or Animals
- Anxious or Destructive Behavior
- Abusive Language or Play with Friends
- Withdrawing From Friends, Family, or Caregivers
- Extreme Apprehensiveness or Vigilance
- Flinching Easily or Avoiding Touch

The consequences of Childhood Sexual Abuse can have a serious impact on physical and mental health. Hyper-sexuality or sex addiction is also more likely to occur in survivors of Childhood Sexual Abuse. In some individuals, food addiction and other eating disorders—such as anorexia and bulimia—may also be triggered by sexual abuse.

Like with adult Sexual Assault, the long-term effects of sexual abuse in childhood include PTSD, depression, eating disorders, sexual dysfunction, substance abuse, obsessive behavior, and suicidal ideation and threats. The shame spiral of untreated sexual trauma can last for months or years, affecting a survivor's everyday life while making future relationships and intimacy feel impossible

It is also linked to higher rates of depression, Post-Traumatic Stress Disorder, substance use, and risky sexual behaviors.

Re-victimization is also likely for a survivor of Childhood Sexual Abuse. For instance, females exposed to sexual abuse as children are two to thirteen times more likely to experience sexual abuse again as adults[40].

In addition, someone who was sexually abused as a child is two times more likely to experience non-sexual domestic abuse by a future partner.

EMOTIONAL ABUSE

This is one of the hardest forms of abuse to recognize because of its subtle and manipulative nature. With Emotional Abuse, survivors develop anxiety, irrational guilt, negative self-talk, perfectionism, irritability, codependency, and self-destructive behavior.

In Emotional Abuse, the aggressor uses shame, Gaslighting, and isolation with threats of abandonment as leverage to control and manipulate another person. Consistent exposure to Emotional Abuse can undermine a person's self-worth and take away their agency.

> Abuse can happen within families, friendships, and romantic partners. The people closest to the survivor with the most private access to them are the aggressors.

In the end, the survivor feels trapped. They are afraid to leave the relationship and, at the same time, they're too wounded to continue to endure the relationship. The cycle will continue to repeat itself until something is done.

Let's take a closer look at the weapons of Emotional Abuse.

GASLIGHTING

Gaslighting falls under the categories of emotional and mental abuse.

The term Gaslighting comes from the movie *Gaslight* [41] (1944) which was based on the 1938 Victorian thriller *Gaslight*, written by the British novelist and playwright Patrick Hamilton[42]. (**Spoiler Alert**) In both versions we see a woman being slowly manipulated by her husband into believing that she is going insane. This is done so that he can have her committed and steal her inheritance.

Dr. Robin Stern coined the term "gaslight effect" in her 2007 book The Gaslight Effect: How to Spot and Survive the Hidden Manipulation Others Use to Control Your Life[43].

"In the vernacular, the phrase 'to gaslight' refers to the act of undermining another person's reality by denying facts, the environment around them, or their feelings. Targets of Gaslighting are manipulated into turning against their cognition, their emotions, and who they fundamentally are as people."

Gaslighting is a way of invalidating the survivor. Wearing them down until they no longer have the will to fight.

It is done slowly, through systematic manipulation, which leads the survivor to question their own reality.

According to the National Domestic Violence Hotline,[44] techniques a person may use to gaslight someone include:

- **Countering**: Questioning the survivor's memory of events, especially when the survivor has an accurate account.

  "Are you sure that's what happened? You know you have a terrible memory."

- **Withholding**: Refusing to engage with the survivor in order to control the narrative.

  (The silent treatment. Stonewalling.)

- **Trivializing**: Belittling or disregarding of the other person's feelings.

  "You're too sensitive. Why do you always have to blow up over little things?"

- **Denial**: Denial of an event, pretending nothing happened, or accusing the survivor of making things up.

  "I don't know what you're talking about. That's not the way things went down."

- **Diverting**: Changing the focus of a discussion and questioning the survivor's credibility.

  "Where did you get that idea? Did your friend put you up to this? You know they hate me."

While anyone can experience Gaslighting, it is especially common in intimate relationships and in social interactions where there is an imbalance of power.

Survivors of Gaslighting often find it difficult to realize they are experiencing abuse.

They may not question the abusive person's behavior because the one doing the Gaslighting is in a position of authority, or because the survivor feels reliant on them.

PERSONAL EXPERIENCE

My husband used to hate going out to dinner, saying he preferred my home cooking instead. He'd get off work and just want to sit down and relax. I'd get off work and also just want to sit down and relax with a meal. To me that meant take out, to him that meant me cooking and plating a meal for him.

So I tried to set up dinner dates with friends and family as a way to coax him out of the house at dinner time instead. He claimed this was a great idea and would take care of it for me, because I was so busy. He would tell our friends to meet us on Tuesday at 5pm. He would tell me we were going to meet them on Wednesday at 6pm. He would get home late on Tuesday, and just wasn't very hungry. On Wednesday, we were always stood up, or he would say they contacted him and had a last minute emergency. When I would talk to them about it later they would say how sorry they were to have missed me. After months of constantly being rejected and snubbed, I wasn't so keen on eating out anymore. I would rather stay in and be depressed and cook whatever was available no matter how tired I was. It was less painful to not go out than to go out and be rejected by the people I cared about.

It was only later that I found out he was telling our friends and family that I didn't come out because I was too tired, busy, depressed, or unwell to make it. My family started pulling away, thinking I needed time and space. I went out less and less because I was so sad/mad about always being stood up. When I inevitably found out that they had been told a different date/time, he insisted that I was remembering it wrong, or he told me the right time and they were wrong, or that we did actually go and he even had a story to tell about the dinner because he had been there, or that I was the one who insisted we go on the wrong date.

For weeks, I thought I was losing my mind and was constantly double-checking everything. He used that to convince me that something was wrong with me, and that was why I was wrong about the dinner dates that I had learned were set up so that I wouldn't be able to attend with my friends.

Common Signs You Have Been a Survivor of Gaslighting Include:

- Feeling confused and constantly second-guessing yourself
- Having trouble making simple decisions
- Frequently questioning if you are being too sensitive
- Becoming withdrawn or unsociable
- Constantly feeling the need to apologize to the abusive person
- Defending or making excuses for the abusive person's behavior
- Feeling hopeless, joyless, worthless, or incompetent

ISOLATION WITH THREATS OF ABANDONMENT

Isolation is extremely effective, subtle, and difficult to detect. Keeping someone, through manipulation or intimidation, from friends, family, peers, and their own independent activities removes that person's social safety net, leaving them reliant on their abuser.

Isolation—The abuser slowly severs all emotional ties except the one to him/her.

Threats of abandonment—A form of emotional manipulation that uses a person's fear of isolation as a weapon.

Some of the ways an abuser can isolate their survivor:

- **Causing a division with family and friends**

  The abuser may question the validity or necessity of the survivor's relationships to drive a wedge between the survivor and their social network.

  "I can't believe your best friend did that. You don't need friends like that."

  "Your mother is too nosey. You're an adult. You don't need to check in with her every day."

- **Preventing the survivor from making new friends by being jealous**

  The abuser leads the survivor to believe he/she loves him/her and wants to protect him/her from people who do not really care about them.

  "I don't want you hanging out with them. They are just trying to steal you away from me."

  "You care more about your friends than me, don't you?"

- **Preventing the survivor from joining the community through manipulation**

  Isolating the survivor from the others ensures the survivor will remain oblivious to the abuse, because they are not able to filter their perception through their social network.

  > *"You spend so much time at the gym. I never get to see you. It's like you don't want to be around me anymore. Is that what you want, to get away from me?"*
  >
  > *"I don't like it when you go out after work with your friends."*

- **Dominating every part of the survivor's daily life**

  The abuser infiltrates every part of the survivor's life, including their home, online social media presence, and banking or finances.

  At this stage, they employ Gaslighting and infantilizing by treating them like a child who needs help to manage every aspect of their day-to-day life. This is done under the guise of helping, when in reality, they are tightening their grip.

Once they have control of everything, the survivor is unable to escape.

PHYSICAL ISOLATION

This is a more extreme step. The abuser will move the survivor away from everything the survivor knows and loves.

In this case, the survivor is completely cut off from their social support network.

Once isolation is established, the abuser is free to use threats of abandonment to control their survivor, knowing they have nothing to fall back on.

PERSONAL EXPERIENCE

My husband withheld intimacy from me from the day we were married. I spent my honeymoon watching him play video games while he ignored me. That should have been my first clue to his emotional unavailability. But I was young and thought we were in love. It would take years for me to realize the truth that he was incapable of actual love.

My needs and desires were not important, but when he decided he wanted sex, there was no saying no. The act was done when he wanted and how he wanted.

He demanded oral sex, but made sure I knew he would never return the act because I was disgustingly feminine. The natural lubricant that my body produced for sex was gag-worthy. Periods were just unmentionable.

At the same time, he would blame me for the lack of intimacy in our relationship whenever I would try to express my concern over it, saying that I put too much pressure on him, or that he was tired of being the one to initiate (which was never the case).

By some miracle, I got pregnant, but it tragically ended in miscarriage. It absolutely devastated me. I called my husband at his work and told him what was happening. He seemed annoyed that I would disturb his work for something like that. and gruffly told me, "So go to the hospital."

At the hospital, they confirmed the miscarriage. I was a mess. My husband refused to come home from work, so I spent the day at a friend's house crying on her couch.

61

When my husband got home, he went straight to playing video games.

I curled up next to him, still crying, which seemed to annoy him further. He turned to me and said: "If you're just going to cry like that, go into the other room. I'm trying to enjoy the rest of my day and you're ruining it."

In the following days/weeks, whenever he would catch me being upset, he would make a show about how annoyed he was with my behavior and say something like: "These things happen. Get over it."

I'd like to say that was a one-off occurrence, but his complete apathy toward my needs continued. Not long after, I became pregnant again, but my happiness was overshadowed by my sister's battle with cancer. I was eight months pregnant when she, sadly, passed away.

When we got the news that she wasn't going to make it, my husband and I were three hours away. He was reluctant to go because he didn't want to drive, so I drove the whole way to the hospital.

While we were there in the waiting room, he played on his phone and often commented on how bored he was. When I went in to see my sister, he didn't even come with me. She was hooked up to breathing machines and monitors. The hospital was only keeping her alive for my family to say goodbye.

When they pulled the plug, my husband was standing in the corner of the hospital room, playing a game on his phone. My dad and my brother held me as we watched my sister pass. On the drive home, he complained about how my dad was an asshole for not hugging him, and how I was a selfish bitch for not making sure my family tended to him while my sister was dying.

I know people don't handle grief in the same way, so I tried to let it slide. But, even weeks later, if my husband

caught me crying over my sister's passing, he would remind me how he thought "she was a bitch anyway," and
told me to keep my tears to myself. He didn't allow me to
reach out to my family for support because of "how they
treated him" that day.

The baby came soon after, and caring for her became
my focus. For a moment, we were a happy family. He even
had a new job prospect that would take us to a different
city.

I let him take our only car to drive out there while I
(only a few weeks postpartum) packed up the entire house
and got ready to move.

A few days after he left, his ex-girlfriend reached out
to me with screenshots of conversations he had been having with her for almost a year. He expressed his desire to
rekindle their relationship and even requested she come to
his temporary apartment to "fool around."

I called and confronted him immediately, but rather
than deny it or attempt to cover up what he was doing, he
claimed "this never would have happened if you had just
been a good wife."

In the stunned silence that followed, he asked me if I
wanted him to leave. It wasn't a genuine question, especially with the threatening tone he'd used to ask it.

Despite the betrayal, I still loved him, and we had just
had a child together. I couldn't destroy our family when it
had just begun.

I told him no, I didn't want him to leave.

I wish I could go back in time and change my answer.
While it had come from a place of love, he had proven to
me that he was truly incapable of the emotion.

He told me that if I wanted him to be faithful, I had to
be a better wife.

Signs of abuse include:

- Constant Criticism and Judgmental Behavior That Leads to Shame
- Gaslighting
- Controlling Behavior
- Isolating From Friends and Family
- Extreme Jealousy

Healing from abuse is a challenging process. The first step is to recognize the problem, and that is why we are going over the various types of trauma here. In later sections, we will take a deep dive into your therapy options.

THE BOTTOM LINE

Emotional Abuse can happen within family systems, friendships, and romantic partners. The people closest to the survivor, with the most private access to them, are the aggressors. With Emotional Abuse, survivors develop anxiety, irrational guilt, negative self-talk, perfectionism, irritability, codependency, and self-destructive behavior.

SEXUAL ASSAULT

Trigger Warning: Sexual Assault is a particularly nasty type of trauma that, sadly, many women are familiar with. It refers to a range of unwanted behavior, coercion, and forceful sexual contact. This includes rape, attempted rape, and or unwanted physical contact.

Sexual violence has long-term effects on the survivor. It creates high levels of stress, anger, guilt, shame, body image issues, and decreased self-esteem:

- 94% of women who are raped experience symptoms of PTSD during the two weeks following Sexual Assault.
- 70% of Sexual Assault survivors experience moderate-to-severe distress, a larger percentage than for any other violent crime.
- 30% of women report symptoms of PTSD 9 months after the Sexual Assault.
- 33% of women who have been sexually assaulted contemplate suicide.
- 13% of women who have been sexually assaulted attempt suicide.

Sexual Assault refers to sexual contact or behavior that occurs without explicit and freely given consent of the survivor. Some forms of Sexual Assault include:

- Attempted rape
- Unwanted sexual touching or non-consensual penetration of the body
- Being forced to perform sexual acts or participate in penetration of the perpetrator's body

The FBI defines rape as:[45]
Rape (revised definition): Penetration, no matter how slight, of the vagina or anus with any body part or object, or oral penetration by a sex organ of another person, **without the consent** of the survivor. (This includes the offenses of rape, sodomy, and Sexual Assault with an object, as converted from data submitted via the National Incident-Based Reporting System.)

Regarding Consent[46]:

- **The term consent means, "a freely given agreement to the conduct at issue by a competent person."**

  An expression of lack of consent through words or conduct means there is no consent.

  A current or previous dating or social or sexual relationship by itself or the manner of dress of the person involved with the accused in the conduct at issue does not constitute consent.

- **A sleeping, unconscious, or incompetent person cannot give consent.**

  Lack of verbal or physical resistance does not constitute consent.

- **A person cannot give consent while under threat or in fear.**

  Submission resulting from the use of force, threat of force, or placing another person in fear does not constitute consent.

We threw a lot of terms and statistics at you, and you may be feeling a bit overwhelmed at the moment, but this is a subject so pervasive in the lives of women, it has to be understood.

Remember, we want you to arm you with the facts because knowledge is power. It can mean the difference between getting the help you need or exacerbating your trauma through Medical Gaslighting (more on that later).

The trauma of being sexually assaulted can leave the survivor feeling scared, ashamed, alone, and potentially plagued by nightmares and flashbacks.

66

A survivor of Sexual Assault can feel like the world isn't a safe place any longer; faith in humanity is shattered and the personal sense of self-worth is diminished. Short-term effects include shock, fear, anxiety, confusion, and withdrawal.

Many survivors blame themselves for what happened. They feel dirty or consider themselves as "damaged goods."

PERSONAL EXPERIENCE

I was nineteen when I was raped by my first husband. I grew up in a Christian household and believed in waiting until marriage for sex. My first husband (boyfriend at the time) worked graveyard shifts and would come to my apartment in the morning when he was done working. Normally, he would cuddle me in bed while I slept, until my alarm went off for me to go to work.

One morning, I woke up to him on top of me, penetrating me. It was incredibly painful. I screamed and shoved him off the bed.

I felt violated, dirty, confused, and scared. I distinctly remember thinking. "Can you even be raped by your boyfriend?"

Despite being in a lot of pain from the encounter, I didn't know what to do. I loved him. You don't report people you love to the police. Even if I did report him, he was my boyfriend. Who would take me seriously?

I remember curling up in a ball on the corner of my bed trying to process what had just happened while he lamented about what a "piece of shit" he was for what he'd just done to me.

When his self-deprecation didn't reach me, he got up

and moved like he was about to leave and said that he was going to go kill himself. The thought of him killing himself over my reaction frightened me and I ended up comforting him despite my own emotional state.

For a brief moment, it felt like we were both in the same place. He had made a terrible mistake, which he regretted, while I struggled with the fact that the sacred marriage I'd been saving myself for was gone. But we still had each other. We could get past this.

During the weeks following that event, my boyfriend would randomly bring it back up. At first, I thought it was because he felt some kind of lingering guilt, but as he would say that it was fine and that I didn't need to feel unworthy, in the same breath would remind me that no man would want me since I was no longer a virgin.

"Whoring around" wasn't acceptable in our church community. The type of man that I would want as my husband would see me as a disgusting person for having been intimate before marriage.

What I had assumed was his guilt turned out to be manipulation. Through shaming me, he convinced me that he was the best I could ever hope to get, and if I wanted to make it right in the eyes of God, I had to marry him.

Left with no other choice, I became a teenage bride.

Here are some Sexual Assault statistics in the U.S. from the National Sexual Violence Resource Center for Adult women:

- 1 in 5 women in the U.S. have been exposed to some form of Sexual Assault in their lifetime.
- 43.6% of women (nearly 52.2 million) have experienced some form of sexual violence in their lifetime.

- A majority of female survivors of completed or attempted Sexual Assault first experienced such victimization early in life, with 81.3% (nearly 20.8 million survivors) reporting that it first occurred prior to age 25.

- Among female survivors of completed or attempted Sexual Assault, 43.2% (an estimated 11.0 million survivors) reported that it first occurred prior to age 18, with 30.5% (about 7.8 million survivors) reporting that their first victimization occurred between the ages of 11 and 17, and 12.7% (an estimated 3.2 million survivors) at age 10 or younger.

- Approximately 1 in 6 women (16.0% or an estimated 19.2 million women) experienced Sexual Coercion (e.g., being worn down by someone who repeatedly asked for sex, or sexual pressure due to someone using their influence or authority) at some point in their lifetime.

- More than a third of women (37.0% or approximately 44.3 million women) reported unwanted sexual contact (e.g. groping) in their lifetime.

- In the U.S., over 1 in 3 (36.4% or 43.6 million) women have experienced sexual or physical violence, and/or stalking by an intimate partner during their lifetime.

- Over one-third of women (36.4% or 43.5 million) have experienced psychological aggression by an intimate partner during their lifetime. [4748]

Long-term effects include PTSD, depression, eating disorders, sexual dysfunction, substance abuse, obsessive behavior, and suicidal ideation. This shame spiral of untreated sexual trauma can last for months or years, affecting a survivor's everyday life while making future relationships and intimacy feel impossible.

Let's take a pause again for another important statement.

What you're experiencing is a normal reaction to trauma.
These are symptoms, not reality.
You are not damaged.
What happened was not your fault.
You deserve to heal.

SPOUSAL RAPE

While we are on the topic of Sexual Assault, we would be remiss if we did not take the time to specifically focus on Spousal Rape and Sexual Coercion.

This one might feel personal to some of you reading this, because it is the most common form of rape that adult women experience.

Though Sexual Assault is recognized as a crime, the idea of sexually assaulting one's spouse can be seen as a contradiction in terms. Throughout history, most societies have treated a woman's sexuality as a commodity that belongs to the woman's husband once vows are said.

The legal and ethical foundation of this in our culture can be traced back to statements made by Sir Matthew Hale, Chief Justice in 17th century England[4950].

"But the husband cannot be guilty of a Sexual Assault committed by himself upon his lawful wife, for by their mutual matrimonial consent and contract the wife hath given up herself in this kind unto the husband which she cannot retract."

In 1970, anti-rape movements argued for elimination of the spousal exemption. (Yes... you read that right. It has only been in the last 50 years that changes have been made.) In 1993, Spousal Rape finally became a crime in all 50 states; however, many states still treat Spousal Rape as different from other rapes, providing exemptions, loopholes, or simply looking at it as a lesser degree of crime, which results in more lenient penalties.

> Because of this, and the belief that, "what happens in the bedroom, between husband and wife, is a private matter," men forcing their wives to have sex, even when it is against her will was not included in the definition of rape until recently.

Spousal Rape is not a rare occurrence.

According to the National Coalition Against Domestic Violence, between 14% and 25% of women are sexually assaulted by intimate partners during their relationship.[51] According to one study, Spousal Rape is four times more common than Sexual Assault by a stranger[52].

> For many women, Spousal Rape is referred to as "doing your wifely duties," even when unwilling, and falls under a few of our trauma categories: Sexual Abuse, Domestic Violence, & Emotional Abuse.

The WHO, on behalf of the U.N. Interagency working group on violence against women, found that worldwide, over a quarter of women aged 15-49 years have been subjected to physical and/or sexual violence by their intimate partner at least once in their lifetime.

This form of abuse is not a one-time, isolated event:

71

- It typically is part of a pattern of emotional or physical abuse.
- It is often not reported due to the relationship between the perpetrator and survivor.
- It is often endured due to financial or familial dependency upon the perpetrator.

Spousal Rape walks hand-in-hand with Sexual Coercion.

"Sexual Coercion is when someone manipulates you into unwanted sexual activity through non-physical means," says Elizabeth L. Jeglic Ph.D.[53], professor of psychology at John Jay College of Criminal Justice, and sexual violence prevention expert.

According to the CDC National Intimate Partner and Sexual Violence Survey (2010), about 1 in 8 women (13%) reported experiencing sexual coercion from an intimate partner, which translates to more than 15 million women in the U.S..[54]

Sexual Coercion looks like:

- Repeatedly asking for sex—wearing a person down
- Lies and promises in exchange for sex
- Being reminded of obligation as a spouse or partner
- Threatening to go elsewhere for sex if it is not given
- Threatening to terminate the relationship if sex is not given
- Threatening violence if sex is not given
- Giving drugs or alcohol to lower inhibitions
- Withholding necessities until sex is given
- Guilt tripping, claiming sex is owed due to previous favors given or money spent

A majority of women who have unwanted sex with their partners do so out of a sense of obligation.

Though Spousal Rape is technically a crime, socially, it is still widely seen as a "wifely duty" to provide sexual satisfaction to a spouse.

Women feel pressured into sex to keep the peace within their relationship. This is especially true for women with children who take on the roles of homemaker and rely on their husbands for financial support.

Legally, there is a thin line between Sexual Coercion and rape, but the reality is, if you don't want to have sex and agree because you feel obligated or to avoid potential consequences, you aren't consenting voluntarily. Non-consensual sex is rape.

The law, however, leaves a messy gray area up to interpretation, and because of this, women often do not define their experiences as Sexual Assault. This makes them less likely to report it or seek outside assistance.

When women do finally reach out and seek some kind of assistance for Spousal Rape, more often than not, they find no help from their support networks including family, friends, health care providers, or religious advisers. This exacerbates feelings of vulnerability, shame, rejection, and abandonment, making PTSD a common outcome.

PERSONAL EXPERIENCE

I endured years of being unhappy in my marriage and giving in to coercion when it became essential to keeping the peace, before I sought help to escape.

While I loved him as a person, and wanted to honor our vows and keep our family together, I had no sexual desire toward my husband. Our marriage had been on the decline for years and I had slowly lost all attraction to him.

Still, men have their needs, right? After a while, he would make the request, giving me two choices.

I could just get it over with, or I could say no. The latter would eventually end in an argument. I know it hurt him to be rejected, and that was not my intention. I did still have love in my heart for him. I just had no desire (thanks to other issues in our relationship). However, the constant pressure to perform, when I had no physical desire or attraction to him, just to avoid a fight, became too much of a strain.

It sounds just as bad as it felt, I assure you. While I knew it was hurting him, I was hurting too. Imagine being touched or fondled by someone you're not attracted to. That shiver that just ran down your spine as you cringed. Yeah. That's it. Only I was feeling that every time the man I was supposed to love touched me. So, not only was I put off, I also felt the guilt of knowing I was causing damage to him at the same time. Not a great place to be in.

I began to actively avoid situations where he might try to initiate sex. I stopped taking showers at night, opting to do it during the day when my husband was at work to avoid him trying to join me and initiate "a quickie." I would avoid sitting next to him on the couch so he wouldn't be tempted to touch me. I would find reasons to be out of the house, scheduling kids plenty of play dates to keep us out all day or night so we'd be exhausted by the time we came home. I would make up endless excuses, claiming headaches, stomach cramps, or being on my period, to avoid being harassed for sex.

There was a regularity to the cycle of his efforts to initiate sex. I could always tell when he was about to come have "the talk" with me. He always wanted to discuss the reasons I was not willing to have sex with him, so he could refute them, as if that were a form of foreplay.

But, despite the numerous times I explained myself, it wasn't enough for me to be honest. The truth was that I did not want to have sex, not with him, not with anyone. I wasn't even engaging in self-satisfaction at that point. That was how put off I had become, and pressuring me made the prospect of it that much more unappealing.

There were times I even suggested he could cheat, if only to let him satisfy his needs and allow me some peace, but that was unacceptable. Until I met his needs, I would not have peace.

My lack of desire for sex was unfathomable to him. Sex was a normal human desire. I should have been happy that he found me sexually attractive, and eager to reciprocate. The times I relented left me feeling dirty and shameful. I had said no, but it didn't matter because he was going to get what he wanted.

At one point, he even went as far as to tell me, "You don't want it because it has been so long since you've had it. You just need to force yourself to get the juices flowing. Once it becomes routine again, you'll want it more." That Freudian-style psychobabble was what turned our talks into shouting matches.

We began arguing so much that our kids were beginning to take notice. There was one point where I realized my son would start acting crazy if he spotted us in a room together. It was as if he was creating a diversion to prevent us from arguing, and that was when I finally hit my limit.

I went to my family, asking for support so I could leave my toxic marriage. I explained to my parents what was happening, revealed our private sexual dysfunctions, and how I was feeling pressured to perform even after clearly stating I was unwilling.

I was not in a good financial position, and the reality was, I could not stand on my own two feet at that time. I *did not have a steady income. My kids were still young and would require a sitter if I couldn't be home with them. I had, for all intents and purposes, been a homemaker with occasional side-gigs for personal spending money during the years of my marriage. My potential job prospects, reentering the workforce after so many years, were few and far between.*

Getting out of the marriage was not an easy decision, and I was counting on my family to be there in my time of need. They were supposed to love unconditionally and support me in troubled times, right? That's what family is for, or so they say. All I needed was a little help to escape and some time to get on my feet.

Rather than find helpful and loving support from my family, I was told to "play nice for the good of my children," and "I was being selfish for wanting to tear my family apart because I was unhappy in my marriage."

I felt utterly betrayed. My own mother twisted the situation around on me, using my children as ammunition. She accused me of being a bad mother. How could I willingly put my children through the trauma of a messy divorce? Why couldn't I just do what my husband wanted? She all but told me was to, "Lay down and take it."

When I needed them the most, my family rejected me. I was labeled as selfish for not wanting to be forced into unwanted sexual acts just to appease my husband's desires.

Read that again.

Is that the world we live in? A world where a woman, attempting to retain her bodily autonomy, is seen as selfish and worthy of ridicule. I guess being a woman means you are damned if you do want to have sex, and damned if you don't want to have sex. That is the message I am getting. There was no winning.

With no support from my family, I did have to play nice. I wasn't in a financial position to do anything else. It took me almost a year to get myself to a place where I could leave my husband and support my children. I had to "play nice," as instructed, going to marriage counseling as a stop gap to give me time to save money and get my business running to a point where I was earning enough to survive on. During that time, my parents made continued attempts to push their agenda of keeping me and my now ex-husband together. I was repeatedly reminded of how little my feelings mattered to them and how disappointed they were in my continued goal of ending the marriage.

It was not an easy year to endure, and had I been given the support I needed, I wouldn't have had to endure it. But I did eventually find my exit.

To this day, as a single mother of three, I operate on survival mentality. After being denied the support of family, essentially cutting off any safety net that social support might have provided, I struggle with worries about finances and keeping a roof over me and my children's heads.

There is no time for me to process the trauma of my toxic marriage, the betrayal of my family, or the deep sense of distrust I now have in others thanks to the rejection I endured for trying to do the right thing. Every waking moment revolves around making sure everyone's needs are met while ensuring there is money coming in to keep a roof over our heads.

I have no space to allow for any new meaningful relationships to begin, and sex is still a topic I'm completely averse to. Responsibilities come first, and because of that, it may be years before I have the time and resources to devote to healing.

That story is far from the worst, but it is one among the many that happens every year in the U.S.

Survivors of Spousal Rape are exposed to multiple instances of their trauma and suffer long-term effects psychologically because of this. On top of that, survivors often have to deal with ongoing relationships with their abuser, especially if they have children.

Due to the intimate nature of the abuse they endured, survivors may also struggle to reconcile genuine feelings of affection for their abuser, which is separate from their trauma over the abuse.

Typical long-term psychological effects of Spousal Rape include sleeping disorders, eating disorders, depression, intimacy problems, negative self-images, sexual dysfunction, substance abuse, and PTSD.

GUILT AND SHAME FOLLOWING SEXUAL TRAUMA

There is often a lot of secrecy surrounding sexual trauma. Survivors who come forward are often ignored or made to feel like they did something wrong. Some are even warned to keep their experience quiet. People often blame the survivor, suggesting things they "should" or "should not" have done.

This leads survivors to internalize, creating Toxic Shame (see Emotional Abuse) following the act.

Let's dispel a few myths about Sexual Assault:

Myth: You can spot a rapist by the way they look or act.

Fact: There's no way to identify a rapist. Many appear completely normal, friendly, charming, and non-threatening. In fact, most perpetrators are known to the survivor. [55]

- Approximately 8 out of 10 Sexual Assaults are committed by someone known to the survivor, such as with intimate partner sexual violence or acquaintance (date) rape.
- Perpetrators of acquaintance rape are not limited to a date, they can be anyone known to the survivor.

Myth: You must not have thought it was that bad if you didn't fight back.

Fact: *Fight, Flight, Freeze, and Tend-and-Befriend (See How Trauma Is Defined) are all normal responses to a traumatic situation. During a Sexual Assault, it's extremely common to freeze. In a crisis, the brain and body shut down in shock, making it difficult to move, speak, or think.*

Myth: People who are raped "ask for it" by the way they dress or act.

Fact: *Rape is a crime of opportunity. Studies show that rapists choose survivors based on their vulnerability, not on how sexy they appear or how flirtatious they are. Refer to the definition of consent. If it was not given, it was never "asked for," and is considered rape.*

Myth: It's not rape if you've had sex with the person before.

Fact: *Prior instances of dating, past intimacy, or other acts like kissing do not give someone consent to increased or continued sexual contact. If your spouse, partner, or lover coheres or forces sex against your will, it's rape.*

THE BOTTOM LINE

Sexual Assault or Childhood Sexual Abuse is a crime against your person. It can have lasting effects if left untreated.

There is hope. Recovery is possible and we will talk about treatment options in a later chapter.

DOMESTIC ABUSE

Domestic Abuse, also known as Domestic Violence or Intimate Partner Violence, is a behavioral pattern rooted in dominance that is used to gain or maintain control over a partner. This dominance pattern extends to any relationships between family members (including children and elders) and romantic partners (pretty much anyone living under the same roof).

When most people think of Domestic Abuse, they often think of the violent element, but it's not only physical violence.

This form of abuse also includes emotional, financial, and sexual abuse, which you may recall are the initial three types of trauma we covered in this chapter.

It's pretty clear to see the overlapping elements here. Domestic Abuse is essentially a systematic application of various traumas.

Since we have already covered those traumas in previous sections, we are going to look at the application of them in this section.

According to the National Coalition Against Domestic Violence:

- On average, nearly 20 people per minute are physically abused by an intimate partner in the U.S.
- 1 in 3 women have experienced some form of physical violence by an intimate partner. This includes a range of behaviors (e.g., slapping, shoving, pushing).
- 1 in 4 women have experienced severe physical violence (e.g., beating, burning, strangling) by an intimate partner in their lifetime.
- 1 in 10 women have been raped by an intimate partner.
- Women between the ages of 18-24 are most commonly abused by an intimate partner.
- 1 in 15 children are exposed to intimate partner violence each year, and 90% of these children are eyewitnesses to this violence.
- On a typical day, there are more than 20,000 phone calls placed to domestic violence hotlines nationwide.[56]

Domestic Abuse involves an imbalance of power within a relationship. The abuser uses intimidating words, behaviors, or actions to control their partner. Incidents of abuse are rarely isolated events. Control is a fluid concept and, because of this, it must be established and constantly maintained. Which, of course, means that, over time, the abuse will often escalate in frequency and severity.

Abusers are often concerned with image. Remember that the core of Domestic Abuse is the imbalance of power within a relationship. Abusers want to be the top dog. To do that, they must appear powerful and in control.

This means that in public, the abuser often comes across as charming.

It is only in private that the true nature is revealed. This leads to situations where a survivor has trouble reaching out for support, because their abuser appears as an upstanding member of society. More on that later.

With Domestic Abuse, the abuse is done in private.

In 1979, Lenore Walker[57] published *The Battered Woman* in which she proposed a cycle of abuse in relationships based on similar patterns of abuse in 1,500 female survivors she interviewed.

While her proposed cycle of abuse does help to illustrate common patterns of abusive behavior in relationships, it has some limitations due to its simplistic portrayal of abuse patterns. Still, it is a good base to start from.

Walker's cycle involves 3-4 stages:

- **First** is the tension-building phase

  In this phase, the abuser is edgy. Tension begins to build up. They feel antsy and get irritated at the slightest thing. This is where the survivor may feel like they are walking on eggshells and may try to placate their abuser.

- **Second** is the actual explosion

  This is where the physical, emotional, and sexual abuse typically occurs.

- **Third** is the honeymoon phase

  The abuser may be sorry and lavish their partner with gifts or affection. Or, they may act like nothing happened and hope their partner will let it slide. They may also act overly guilty and make grand promises to never do it again. The purpose here is to make sure the abuse never gets reported. The abuser will do their best to convince the survivor that the worst is over.

- **Fourth** (not always included) Calm

  This is simply a period of calm before the cycle starts again. Life within the relationship is easy. This allows the survivor to be lulled into a sense of false security.

The reality is, the tension always builds again, and thus the cycle continues. The cycle may be fast, and happen with frightening regularity. Or, it could be a slow cycle that happens over months or years.

The bottom line here is that the cycle repeats.

A more modern interpretation of this cycle comes in the form of the Power and Control Wheel[58] (created in 1984 by the Domestic Abuse Intervention Project) which is a more comprehensive breakdown of the tactics which abusers use to establish and maintain control over their partner.

Remember that we said Domestic Abuse is the systematic application of various types of traumas. Physical violence is the action that establishes or reinforces control. This is the one we most often think of when the words domestic violence are thrown around because it results in physical harm. But physical violence does not have to be applied regularly to maintain control. Often, the threat of violence after one or more occurrence is enough. And that is precisely how the more subtle and continual abusive behaviors keep the survivors trapped in their relationship.

Each of the following topics of abuse represents a spoke on the wheel of power and control:

- **Emotional Abuse**

  Using insults, shame, and isolation to undermine a person's self-worth and take away their agency

- **Economic Abuse**

  Restricting access to job and money making a person reliant on the abuser

- **Sexual Abuse**

  Forcing a partner to engage in sex acts when they do not willingly consent

- **Threats**

  Making threats to do something to hurt a person emotionally

  Threatening to leave or end the relationship

  Threatening to take children away or remove visitation access

  Threatening to commit suicide

  Threatening to reveal a private secret

- **Intimidation**

  Creating fear by using looks, actions, gestures, loud voice, smashing things, or destroying property

- **Minimizing**

  Using gaslighting techniques to create blame shifting so the abuser appears innocent while the survivor appears crazy

Many people believe that Domestic Abuse is due to the abuser's loss of control over their behavior, but that couldn't be more wrong.

Abusive behavior is a deliberate choice to assert power and control.

With that in mind, there are some common aspects among abusive people that contribute to this problem:

84

- **Abusers Are Selective in Who They Abuse.**

  Abusers don't insult, threaten, or assault everyone in their life. Abuse is directed toward someone they know they can abuse. In most cases, this someone they have private access to , and over whom they can assert their power and control.

- **Abusers Public and Private Faces Are Very Different.**

  They control themselves in public, waiting until no one else is around to see their abusive behavior.

- **Abusers Can Stop Their Abusive Behavior When it Benefits Them.**

  They are controlled when they need to be (e.g. when the police show up or if company is visiting).

- **Abusers Usually** (but not always) **Direct Their Violent Blows Where They Won't Show.**

  Rather than acting out in a mindless rage, many physically violent abusers aim their attacks where the bruises and marks won't show.

This conflict of appearance with what the public sees versus what the survivor experiences often leads to survivors having problems getting people to believe them when they do finally seek help.

Feeling trapped in the relationship, survivors of Domestic Abuse may try to calm or pacify their abuser in an effort to avoid the abuse, but none of their efforts will stop it.

The only way to end the cycle of abuse is to leave.

According to the National Domestic Violence Hotline[59], it takes an average of 7 attempts for a survivor to successfully leave their abuser. And leaving brings its own problems.

Statistics show the most dangerous time for a survivor is when they are attempting to leave the abusive partner. Feeling trapped is the most common reasons people continue to stay in these abusive relationships. Remember, power and control are the core of Domestic Abuse. Leaving the abuser is a direct challenge to their power. This often causes an escalation of abusive behaviors in order to keep the survivor trapped.

> A survivor's reasons for staying with or returning to their abuser, after an attempt to escape, are complex. In many cases, their reasons are based on the effects of the long-term abuse and its consequences.

Some Common Barriers to Escape:

- **Fear for Their Safety**

  The abusive partner may threaten to hurt or kill them (and their children) if they leave or report the abuse to law enforcement or child protective services.

- **Fear for Children**

  The fear of further damaging children by separating them from a parent. Fear of losing their child due to a custody battle or having to send children into a potential abuse situation during court ordered visitations with the abuser. Fear of the children being used as pawns in further Emotional Abuse.

- **Fear for Pets**

  The fear of losing their pets (family pets and/or emotional support or service animals) due to threats or a custody battle. Fear of their pets being used as pawns in further Emotional Abuse.

- **Financial Dependence on the Abuser**

  If the abusive partner had total control over finances and earned all the household income, the survivor may have no personal assets with which to establish a new home.

- **Lack of a Social Support System**

  Isolation is one of the abuser's tactics to maintain control.

  This systematically removes the survivor's support system, leaving them no one to turn to.

- **Self-Blame**

  Many times, survivors believe that the abusive is somehow their fault. They have a distorted worldview due to the emotional manipulation from their abusive partner, and may feel they deserved what they got.

- **Belief in False Apologies and Promises of Change**

  Some abusers make a good show of looking and sounding remorseful, and can convince the survivor that they have changed and will never hurt them again (they often do).

  This is a common reason for return.

- **Love**

  Survivors may still love their abusers. The relationship was established from a place of love, and even when injured, survivors may still hold on to the love they once had for their abuser.

  This is a common reason for return.

- **Cultural or Religious Reasons**

  Traditional religious institutions almost always prioritize the sanctity of marriages and promote saving relationships. Divorce can be a reason to ban a member from places of worship or bring shame to their family, further isolating a survivor from important social support systems.

THE BOTTOM LINE

Domestic Abuse employs multiple forms of trauma over an extended period of time. This creates a situation where the survivor's physical and emotional health has been severely impaired.

Studies of survivors in domestic violence shelters found that 88% of women were living with PTSD. Before healing can begin, the survivor must first escape. This means finding some form of support and, more importantly, accepting it.

If you are in this situation right now, we urge you to contact the National Domestic Violence Hotline at 1-800-799-SAFE (7233) or visit https://www.thehotline.org/

TRAUMA BONDS

As we showed you in the previous section, leaving an abusive relationship usually isn't as simple as just walking out the door.

Along with concerns about finding a place to live, supporting yourself, and/or struggling to arrange amicable custody schedules for any shared children, it can feel as if you're tied to your previous partner with no way to truly sever that tie. Then, in the small hours as you lay awake in your bed, thoughts of them creep back in.

> Don't throw the book across the room just yet, we're not saying after all that time spent getting away, that you are doomed to go back. But, there is another issue that we have to address.

The emotional attachment, known as a Trauma Bond, develops out of a repeated cycle of abuse, devaluation, and positive reinforcement. You had a front-row seat to both the best and worst your partner had to offer, and more than that, the relationship had most likely been built on the foundation of genuine attraction and love. Those are hard to ignore.

The term Trauma Bonding was coined by Patrick Carnes, PhD, CAS in 1997[60]. Carnes is a specialist in addiction therapy and the founder of the International Institute for Trauma and Addiction Professionals (IITAP). He shared the theory of Trauma Bonding in a presentation called "Trauma Bonds, Why People Bond To Those That Hurt Them."

Many abusive relationships begin with a shower of affection. With NPD (Narcissistic Personality Disorder) the term is called "Love Bombing."

Love bombing refers to a form of emotional manipulation where the suitor "bombs" you with over-the-top amounts of affection, flattery, gifts, and praise early in the relationship.

89

This is done to capture your attention and keep it firmly on them.

> Love bombing, Gaslighting, and Trauma Bonding are all aspects in the same continuum of an abusive relationship.

Your defenses lower as you begin to see them as the perfect mate. How could you not? They say all the right things. It's only been two weeks and they already talk about introducing you to their mother. That expensive piece of jewelry you casually mentioned you loved, they bought it for you.

They spend all their time, energy, and money making you feel like the most special person in the world. The affection and generosity seems too good to be true, but maybe you have finally found "the one," just like in those romance books you secretly read.

The truth is, when an abuser love bombs, it's a very clever trap. Red flag number one is in the extreme nature of the attention and generosity. They move in too fast with too much perfection.

Sure, the beginning of a relationship can feel like a whirlwind, but that getting to know you phase is often awkward and real couples, even those that are head over heels for each other, are going to reveal their negative qualities. Real relationships have a cycle of unintentional missteps and miscommunication as the two love birds incorporate each other into their lives.

To have no initial flaws and missteps, or worse, be the stereotypical flawless knight in shining armor from day one, is about as fake as it gets. You see the perfection they portray, and they see the reflection in your eyes.

They feed off of your love for them, especially if you're dealing with a narcissist.

Still, whatever the reason, you were swept off of your feet and fell madly in love. There's no shame in that. We all want that perfect someone. But you didn't just fall in love, you stumbled right into their trap.

Carnes defined **Trauma Bonding as "dysfunctional attachments that occur in the presence of danger, shame, or exploitation" and considered it one of nine possible reactions to a traumatic situation.**

He surmised that Trauma Bonding occurs due to the way our brains handle trauma and adapt to ensure survival.

Remember, it is our brain's job to keep us alive. Our first response to danger is flight, fight, freeze, or in some cases we tend-and-befriend, also called fawning (more on that in a second).

When you're faced with a sudden shift in your new love's behavior and they turn abusive, the brain sends a warning to the rest of your body. Adrenaline and cortisol (the stress hormones) flood in, jump-starting your survival instinct.

More often than not, the confusion combined with the newly established feelings you've developed for this person, sends you into freeze response.

Emotional attachments are common, if not essential for a Trauma Bond to form[61].

When the abuser snaps out of their rage, they appear horrified at what they have just done. They profess their love, promising never to do it again. Their apology comes with tears, gifts, and extra good behavior.

Trauma Bonding and love bombing are part of the abuse cycle. After experiencing abuse, the manipulating party will often follow it up with love bombing — displays of affection, perhaps also coupled with Gaslighting to make you believe that what you experienced wasn't abuse, or that you somehow deserved it.

Hormones play a powerful role in reinforcing this bond.

Dopamine and Oxytocin are both feel- good hormones that can overpower your brain's warning signals, keeping you locked in the relationship.

Dopamine is strongly associated with pleasure and rewards, and those gifts and sweet gestures your love shows you after the incident of abuse appear like further proof of their commitment to never hurt you again.

Don't believe dopamine is that powerful? How often do you lean on a specific comfort food when you're stressed?

You're thinking about it now, aren't you? Already salivating at the thought of the food that to your brain, represents a reprieve from anxiety, a reward for being strong and adulting.

No shame there. That's your brain functioning as it should. Those reward signals that make us crave a sweet treat in times of stress is a chemical response to the opposite of our feel-good hormones. The brain is always working[62].

Unfortunately, it is that same chemical response that reinforces our desires for things, and occasionally leads to addictions.

In a sense, the cycle of abuse followed by love bombing and gifts can be looked at as the abuser creating an addiction[63] through apologetic reinforcement.

The hormone Oxytocin is essential for human connection, but experiences and interpersonal predispositions complicate oxytocin's social-bonding capabilities. For those with aggressive tendencies, preserving a relationship can mean controlling or dominating the partner with physical and Emotional Abuse.

> Oxytocin, also known as the love hormone, has been touted as the physiological glue that brings humans together. It is released during sexual intimacy, and makes us trust and become attached to one another.

In his book *The Other Side of Normal*, Harvard psychiatrist, Jordan Smoller[64] explains that prior trauma in relationships gives a "negative coloring" to trust and intimacy. Oxytocin is still released when unhealthy relationships form; it just becomes associated with relationship trauma and contributes to unhealthy attachments.

Flush with dopamine after your love's over-the-top apology and promise to never hurt you again, and a little oxytocin-releasing make up sex, our bodies are addicted and our hearts are sympathetic enough to forgive.

It will never happen again, right?

But often, it does. Fast forward a few more cycles. You can't even remember what set them off. It had to be bad for them to rage like that.

The kick your brain gives you to flight, fight, freeze, or fawn, has been hit one too many times to just stand there frozen. Your best bet to stop the abuse is to fawn.

Remember back in chapter 2, when we talked about tending and befriending? Men and women cope with stress differently.

Studies have found that men typically respond to stressful or threatening situations with fight, flight, and sometimes freeze. Women, however, are more likely to respond with tend-and-befriend[65,66].

Tending involves taking care of people.

Befriending is the process of reaching out to people to create a network of support.

In simple terms, women are wired toward protecting, calming, and befriending in stressful situations as a method of diffusing rather than reacting by fight, flight, or freeze.

This biological-behavioral response is at the core of our maternal instinct and stems from primitive reactions to threats, including predators, assaults, natural disasters, and any other threats to self and offspring.

Even as your love strikes, you do everything you can to calm them. You might even start making excuses for them and take the blame for causing their outburst.

Don't you start feeling sorry for yourself. No matter what you're thinking right now, please know you are not to blame.

Believing you caused the abuse or brought it on yourself is the kind of negativity that will keep you locked in the abusive relationship.

**Being on the receiving end of abuse is NEVER your fault,
and you deserve better.**

Trauma Bonding is not only reserved for love relationships. It can also form between:

- A child and their abusive caregiver
- A hostage and kidnapper (though we associate that with Stockholm syndrome)
- A cult leader and their followers

In the face of trauma we can't escape from, our brain does what it can to keep us alive. In this case, that is adapting a placating or fawning approach to diffuse our love's anger and aggression.

After the worst is over, we may realize we're trapped in the relationship, powerless to leave. It's not always bad, however. The abuse comes in cycles, and in those in-between times, you might allow yourself to believe everything is okay.

Your love doesn't always treat you poorly. In fact, sometimes they treat you better than anyone else has.

Trauma Bonds are deeply damaging to your confidence and sense of self. The emotional side of the abuse you've endured leaves you unsure of your feelings or perceptions.

We've mentioned disassociation before (This is a fifty-cent word for disconnection). It is not uncommon to "check out" during the abuse. It is another way your brain helps you to endure.

The exposure to love and approval at different points during the early stages set up a pattern of intermittent reinforcement that has you locked into the relationship in a similar fashion to the powerlessness that a drug addict feels when they're in the throes of withdrawal.

Psychologist B.F. Skinner[67] discovered that, while behavior is often influenced by rewards or punishment, the specific way rewards are doled out can cause that behavior to persist over long periods of time. That behavior would also be less vulnerable to stopping.

Consistent rewards for a certain behavior produce less of that behavior over time than an inconsistent schedule of rewards.

Skinner discovered that rats pressed a lever for food more steadily when they didn't know when the next food pellet was coming than when they always received the pellet after pressing (continuous reinforcement) the lever.

> Just like with the rats, when our brains are randomly rewarded at varying, unpredictable times, we continue to seek those rewards, even if there will never be another.

A childhood history of trauma can make it harder to break Trauma Bonds. People who experienced abuse in childhood often feel drawn to similar relationships in adulthood, since the brain already recognizes the highs and lows of the intermittent reinforcement cycle.

This is the reason why it can be so difficult to extricate yourself from a Trauma Bond, and why it is so important to seek outside help in doing so.

The Impact of Trauma Bonding

The largest and worst impact of Trauma Bonding is that the positive feelings developed for an abuser can lead a person to stay in an abusive situation. That can lead to continued abuse at best, and death at worst[68].

Once separated from the abuser, someone who has

Trauma Bonded to their abuser may experience everything from continued trauma to low self-esteem. One study noted that the impact on self-esteem continued even six months after the separation from the abuser[69].

Additionally, the after-effects of Trauma Bonding can include depression and anxiety. Experiencing Trauma Bonding may also increase the likelihood of an intergenerational cycle of abuse[70].

Plan for Safety

If you are currently in an abusive situation, you should leave it when you have created a safety plan. This involves having somewhere safe to go with support.

If you are in this situation right now, we urge you to contact the National Domestic Violence Hotline at 1-800-799-SAFE (7233) or visit https://www.thehotline.org/

MORAL INJURY

In 1984, the term "Moral Distress" was conceptualized by philosopher Andrew Jameton in his book *Nursing Practice: The Ethical Issues*[71]. He describes the psychological conflict nurses experienced during ethical dilemmas.

"Moral distress arises when one knows the right thing to do, but institutional constraints make it nearly impossible to pursue the right course of action."

In the 1990s, the term "Moral Injury" was coined by psychiatrist Jonathan Shay[72] and colleagues and defined it as,

"A betrayal of what is right by someone who holds legitimate authority in a high stakes situation."

97

In 2009, the term "Moral Injury" was modified by Brett Litz and colleagues[73], adding,

"Perpetrating, failing to prevent, or bearing witness to acts that transgress deeply held moral beliefs and expectations."

Moral Injury research and writing is primarily focused on military Service Members and Veterans; however, as trauma often occurs in a morally complex context, we need to explore its impact on individuals.

In simple terms, it means acting in a way (witnessing, participating, or failing to prevent something) that goes against a person's moral beliefs. Some researchers call these "transgressive acts": experiences that violate (or transgress) acceptable boundaries of behavior.

Moral Injuries don't necessarily involve threats to one's life, instead, they threaten one's deeply held beliefs and trust. Moral Injury is also not classified as a mental illness by the DSM-5; however, the effects of Moral Injury can cause profound feelings of shame and guilt, which result in negative self-talk and beliefs (See Toxic Shame).

A 2018 meta-analysis found that exposure to potentially morally injurious events were significantly associated with Post-Traumatic Stress Disorder, depression, and suicidality[74].

Journalist Diane Silver[75] describes Moral Injury as,

"A deep soul wound that pierces a person's identity, sense of morality, and relationship to society."

No matter where Moral Injury occurs, when our experiences challenge our fundamental core values, it eats away at us. It undermines the trust we have in our self, in others, and the world we live in.

Moral Injury is soul damage, and, because we often can't talk about what happened (for a punishable or prosecutable reason) we resort to punishing ourselves.

Litz et al.'s research[76] found that we punish ourselves by sabotaging or "self-handicapping." This includes social withdrawal, substance use, and self-condemnation.

We can't talk about it, so we isolate.

We stuff our feelings down, jump into a bottle, and become our own most vicious critic. The self-talk is debilitating.

"Only a monster would ____"

"Only an animal would ____"

"It should have been me."

We fill in that blank and play it over and over in our minds.

In describing the difference between guilt and shame, Brené Brown[77] notes that guilt is, "I did something wrong" and shame is, "I am something wrong."

Think of Moral Injury as a full-out existential crisis; one in which we ask the question: what is the meaning of my existence? It is deep, spiritual muck that cuts to the core of our identity, our morality, and our relationships - with ourselves, our family (especially our children), and humanity at large.

With Moral Injury, the trauma and its meaning need to be processed. We need to stare into the belly of the beast and process betrayal, anger, self-loathing, and the desire to self-harm.

INSTITUTIONAL BETRAYAL

This refers to wrongdoings perpetrated by an institution upon individuals who depend on that institution.[78]

This includes any failure to prevent or appropriately respond to wrongdoings perpetrated by members of or within the institution.

Jennifer J. Freyd, PhD is the Professor Emerit of Psychology at the University of Oregon, the Founder and President of the Center for Institutional Courage, a Faculty Affiliate of the Women's Leadership Innovation Lab at Stanford University, and an all-around dynamic human being who coined the term *Institutional Betrayal* in 2008 and has delivered rich research to guide the study.

Institutional Betrayal is a systemic issue that runs rampant in our modern society and comes in many nuanced flavors that can contribute to or exacerbate trauma.

Even if you've never heard of Institutional Betrayal before, you probably heard of DARVO [79] during the #MeToo movement, or maybe even seen it explained on South Park. DARVO[80] stands for "Deny, Attack, Reverse Victim & Offender," and it is an aggressive form of Institutional Betrayal.

When a survivor of Institutional Betrayal attempts to come forward and accuse their aggressor and the result is humiliation or ostracization of that survivor, rather than punishment for the aggressor, this issue becomes compounded by **Social Trauma,** Social pressure, exclusion, humiliation, or rejection that results in symptoms of social anxiety disorder.

The lasting effect of trauma is compounded by who created it, and how negatively the reporting of that trauma was handled.

PERSONAL EXPERIENCE

For years I was brutally beaten by my father. He would use a leather belt to beat my siblings and me. Not one or two licks. Not even ten or fifteen. By the time I was in third grade I was getting twenty-three plus lashes with the belt at full swings. I remember that vividly because he would force us to count out loud.

One morning, the neighbor asked what the screaming was always about. I told them the truth. He looked horrified, then shrugged and got in his truck then left. Even though he didn't do anything, realizing I could tell someone what was happening gave me courage. I stopped trying to hide my ripped up hair and bruises.

I was sent to the school nurse, who asked me what was wrong with my hair. The teacher sent me in for suspected lice. I told the nurse what really happened, how brutally my father beat us, how he picked me up by my hair when I fell, showed her the welts and bruises, even showed her my bloody scalp. She treated my wounds and sent me back to class.

I dawdled at the start of recess and asked my teacher about it. She seemed confused. I didn't have lice, so what was the problem? Tearing up, I told her about the abuse. How the TV said if something bad was happening at home to tell a trusted adult like a teacher or school nurse. She frowned. I still remember that frown, and she asked what I thought she would do about it. I went to recess instead.

I was angry and did not hide it. Over the next few weeks, I didn't do anything wrong, but I was snippy with

101

her. She had enough and sent me to the principal. I ran to the office and excitedly waited to tell someone who was really in charge! Surely he would help. I had fresh welts and some new scabs to show him. My ear was swollen from where the belt had whipped around my head. I had a belt buckle imprint on my lower back.

The principal called me in and asked why I was there. I told him I needed to report abuse at home. I'd been paying extra attention to the PSAs on TV so I could figure out what had gone wrong the first two times I had reported. He asked me to explain, refused to look at my wounds, told me I should try to do better, and to stop giving my teacher a hard time. Then he told me I could go back to class without getting a paddling.

Something in me broke. All the trust and respect I had for school officials was gone. I told him I didn't care about the paddling. Even with the bruises, it wouldn't feel like much in comparison. And I left.

Of course, when I got home I got beat for getting sent to the principal's office, by my mother. Then by my father when he got home. Then again the next morning before school. I went to school on wobbly legs, welts still forming. I told my teacher my parents said I had to apologize for being mean to her. She smiled.

The next year, I tried a different approach. I was given an assignment to write what I hoped would happen before break. I wrote that I wished my parents would divorce. My teacher asked about it. I told her that my father beat me all the time, leaving welts and bruises and punched me and would throw me around by my hair and I wanted to get away from him before he killed me. She looked really disturbed by that and nodded, then gave me a hug. I was so relieved.

The next night, my parents called me out to have a

talk. They held up my paper. I knew I was going to be killed. I was already up to 76 counted lashes. Nearly twice as many as Jesus. I gave them some lie about how we were always broke and on TV the wife got a new house and the dad would take them on trips every weekend. They explained that wasn't what divorce meant, and it didn't work that way and sent me to bed. I thought I had gotten away with it and heard them talking.

They had called my teacher. She told them what I said, I assume. I don't remember much after my father stormed in, a belt in one hand and something large and wooden in the other, except my sister screaming as she got caught in the blows and I tried to move my body over hers to protect her. I was beaten unconscious. My mother called the school and said I was sick for a few days. When it was time to go back, my sister put makeup on me and did my hair to hide the bald spots.

My teacher smiled and welcomed me back, saying she was so grateful everything had been resolved and I really shouldn't lie about such things because claiming abuse was serious and someone could get in trouble. I sat down, rubbed the concealer off on my clothes with spit, and pulled the rubber bands out of my hair.

I never trusted a teacher again, but I also refused to hide what they didn't want to see.

Institutional Betrayal involves active omission (denying events occurred or disbelief of the survivor), retaliation, and, more often than not, continuing betrayal via tolerance for the act that caused the trauma.

Because we are dealing with trauma that is tied to a system that the survivor is bound to, a lack of trust leads to internalizing of the pain. They cannot speak up because it will do them no good.

So their only choice is to develop adaptive strategies that allow them to continue to function. On the outside, this looks like acceptance, leaving the aggressor unchallenged and free to continue traumatizing the survivor.

THE BOTTOM LINE

Institutional Betrayal is a fundamental violation of trust in the person, institution, or system that not only allows the trauma to occur, it also does nothing to prevent future occurrences of that trauma while relying on social conditioning to keep people silent.

MEDICAL TRAUMA

The idea that medical treatment can be traumatic may seem counterintuitive because we often associate medical care with healing, not harming.

The truth is, sometimes, in the service of healing, medical interventions and interactions with medical staff can result in severe Traumatic Stress.

In most cases, the medical professionals are simply trying to do their jobs, but even in life-saving procedures, the feelings of being violated and/or confused can stay with the patient for years.

Considering the potential emotional and psychological distress of an unforeseen diagnosis and the physically invasive nature of some medical procedures—including immobilization;

loss of control; clouded mental function due to shock, anesthesia, or medications; a sense of being dehumanized; and unfamiliar sterile environments filled with unknown faces—it is easy to see how these experiences can create Traumatic Stress.

The big issue with Medical Trauma is that it is subjective.

Two people can have the same medical procedure and view it differently. While one person may have gone through the procedure with no problems, the other might have viewed it as a traumatic experience. This does not mean the procedure itself was traumatic, however, for the person who viewed it this way, they did, in fact, experience trauma.

Let's look at a common medical procedure that a majority of women will experience in their life.

Birth is a procedure, often done in a hospital setting, that is often prepared for. Women go in with expectations and often outline them in the form of a birth plan. If a plan is written, it is usually discussed with the doctor who will be attending the birth.

And yet, when the day comes to have the child, much of the planning and preparation goes out the window. It can be small changes, like not being allowed to have music playing to keep the mother calm, or choosing to have that epidural when they originally said they would abstain.

It can also be extreme changes, like having an induction, the use of forceps, or having an emergency cesarean section.

Even if everything goes according to plan, the experience of being in a hospital can cause distress.

Strange people coming in at all hours of the day and night. Loss of control of bodily functions while doctors and nurses poke, prod, and monitor your nether regions. The lack of agency. If you have an epidural, you might as well be invisible. The nursing staff and doctor will not pay any attention to you until the baby is practically crowning.

PERSONAL EXPERIENCE

I was determined to have my third baby vaginally. My first two were C-sections. I struggled to find a doctor who would allow me to have a vaginal childbirth. When I finally found one, I had to drive an hour each way to get to his office for my many appointments. The same applied to the hospital he had privileges at. It was worth it, in my opinion, to make the sacrifices to have the birth I wanted.

When the day came, I felt great. I went into the hospital ready. I hired a doula[81], knowing I would need a little extra support during the birth. They are specially trained to help mothers through the labor and use massage, movement, and loving support to help keep the mother calm.

I spent hours in labor, doing fine, not needing the epidural. It was going to be a long labor and I remember my doula saying she wanted to pop back to her office to grab a special pillow for me to use. Right after she left the hospital room, my doctor came in. I had been laboring for hours at this point, having come in around 4um after my water had broken.

This was the first time he'd been in to see me since being admitted to the hospital. At the time, it was fine; I was nowhere near ready to have the baby. I expected the normal examination.

What I did not expect was to be told that he required an internal monitor for the baby for all his VBAC (vaginal birth after cesarean) patients. I had no time to absorb the information before he was lubing up his hands to reach in and place it. Yeah. You get the picture?

The monitor did not go in easily, and it took a bit of trial and error to place it. Apparently, I have a backward facing cervix. Lucky for me.

I screamed and cried the whole time he worked to place the damn thing. I was told, matter-of-factly, that if he couldn't place the monitor, I'd have to have a C-section, due to liability reasons (whatever that meant). So I suffered through the pain. When he finished placing the monitor, he left. I wouldn't see him again until delivery.

At that point, I was a blubbering, crying mess. My husband, at the time, might have wanted to help, but he could do nothing to calm me down. All I could do was cry.

When my doula returned, she found me hyperventilating and dry heaving on the hospital bed. She helped calm me down and get me back into the mindset of having my baby.

Had it not been for the doula I had hired, the whole birth could have been traumatic. The nurses ignored my cries. My husband was useless in my time of need. The doctor, who had administered the painful monitor, was completely detached from the pain he had caused.

Thanks to the pain from the monitor, I ended up giving up my hope to have a drug free birth. I got the epidural, which taught me yet another truth about the birth experience I had not been prepared for.

Once that epidural was placed and the numbness kicked in, the hospital staff had no reason to pay attention to me. Even as I became fully dilated and was ready to push, I was told to wait until my doctor got there. An extra hour of waiting, if you'd like to know[82].

It's nothing like the movies. Had I been undedicated,

they wouldn't have been able to put me on hold. Whether that delay in pushing had any effects on the need for vacuum assisted extraction or if it was due to that rear-facing cervix, I can't say. But the delivery was yet another part of the process I had not prepared for.

Nothing I had prepared for matched my experience.

"Trauma is in the eye of the beholder... If a typical clinician looked at their record, they would never dream that the woman could have perceived the birth to be traumatic." explains Cheryl Tatano[83] Beck, DNSc, CNM, FAAN, a distinguished professor at the University of Connecticut's School of Nursing and one of the leading experts on birth trauma.

We're highlighting traumatic birth here, as it is a form of Medical Trauma that many women encounter in their lives. This is not to say it is the only form, and not all women choose to have children, so they will not experience it, but for many, it is an easy one to relate to.

The truth is, any medical procedure has the potential to be traumatic. Even if medical staff are doing their jobs to the best of their abilities, the actions they may have to take can cause trauma for the patient.

Some procedures that can lead to Medical Trauma:

- Giving birth
- Being intubated
- Cancer diagnosis & treatments
- Any form of surgery
- Chronic pain (especially when doctors are unable to diagnose source)
- Chronic illness
- Childhood health issues

The patient's experience of the treatment/procedure is the key takeaway here because Medical Trauma is subjective in nature. However, though subjective, the trauma that a patient experiences can develop clinically significant reactions, such as PTSD, anxiety, depression, and complicated grief[84].

Some examples of experiences that can lead to Medical Trauma:

- Medical Gaslighting
- A medical professional ignored you when you said you were in pain
- You received a lower standard of care
- A medical professional didn't take concerns about your symptoms seriously
- Not being prepared for the experience before undergoing a medical procedure
- Wishes weren't respected in the operating room
- Being separated from a primary support person, like a partner or family member, during your procedure

Medical Trauma is often a related to and can be compounded by the doctor–patient relationship (or lack thereof). This is important. The quality of the doctor–patient relationship can make or break the patient experience. The medical provider is expected to build rapport, earn trust, and communicate care and respect. This allows the patent to feel comfortable with the suggested procedures going forward.

PERSONAL EXPERIENCE

I was shy during my OBGYN appointments for my first child, and the doctor did not take any time to try and make me feel comfortable.

I was blindsided when he asked me to strip down for him to check my cervix. He left the room and gave me a gown to change into, and when he came back, he was impatient with his instructions on how to position myself for him to reach inside of me to check.

He told me to open my knees, and I hesitated. So he pried them apart and shoved his hand up into me. He did that every visit until I had my baby, and I never felt comfortable with him. But, he was the doctor. I had to just trust that he was doing what was best, right?

During the birth, he told me I needed an IV so that he could induce my labor. I expressed my fear of needles and he scoffed, saying, "You're going to have to get over that." Shortly after that, a nurse came in with my birth plan in her hand. She went over every single point saying that what I wanted was fine, but they were going to do whatever they wanted to do, anyway.

I specifically requested that no vacuum or forceps be used on the baby and the nurse said that my preference didn't matter and if the doctor felt the need to use them, he would, despite my requests for alternative actions.

Thankfully, my daughter was born. I thought I had endured the worst of it, but unbeknownst to me, I was bleeding from a third-degree tear that my doctor had failed to properly close.

It wasn't until the epidural wore off, and I attempted to stand and make my way to the bathroom, that anyone realized what was going on.

I fainted in the middle of the room. When I woke up, a nurse was helping me to the bed. She had to call my doctor back in to sew up that last tear.

When they checked my blood pressure, the nurse was shocked and said that it was so low that they needed to keep me longer for observation.

110

I nearly died from blood loss because the doctor didn't sew up a third-degree tear after the birth. Based on what the nurses had said, after the fact, he was being negligent in his care, and it wasn't a simple mistake.

He was the medical professional. He was supposed to know what he was doing. I trusted in that fact, despite all the discomfort I'd had in dealing with him.

If you can't trust the doctor to do their job, who can you trust? The whole ordeal has shattered my opinion of medical professionals.

MEDICAL GASLIGHTING

Gaslighting is the repeated denial of someone's reality in an attempt to invalidate or dismiss them. It is a form of Emotional Abuse.

Medical Gaslighting is when a medical professional downplays or dismisses what a patient is telling them.

This can be traumatic and abusive. This can manipulate the patient into thinking they are exaggerating their own symptoms, or imagining them all together.

When it leads to medical negligence or patients not seeking further help with their symptoms, the results can sometimes be fatal.

Medical Gaslighting typically falls under one of these categories:

- Blaming a patient's symptoms or illness on psychological factors
- Trivializing a patient's symptoms
- Denying a patient's illness entirely

111

Here's what that can look like:

- Disregarding what you tell them, making you think what you have to say isn't important
- Making you feel belittled, silly, or that you are wasting their time
- Does not believe what you are telling them. You and your experience are wrong.
- Minimalizing your symptoms by saying, "it's normal" or "nothing"
- Assumes a diagnosis based on your gender, identity, age, sexuality, ethnicity, or weight, without any further tests
- Blames your symptoms on a mental illness
- Refuses tests or treatments

PERSONAL EXPERIENCE

After my third military deployment, I was not doing well. I couldn't sleep, was drinking too much, I felt frightened all the time, and I was suicidal. I had an outburst at work, and my boss directed me to report to mental health. The psychiatrist I saw was an active duty, male colonel.

I poured my heart out because I knew I needed help – I knew something was wrong, but I didn't know what.

After talking for an hour, this colonel told me he saw I was struggling, "but I can't help you if you're not honest with me."

I was bewildered and he clarified that he could not help me because, "we all know women don't serve in combat."

This was a kick to the jaw on many levels.

He actively undermined my reality by denying facts, my environment, and my feelings.

When a medical or mental health professional blames a patient's illness or symptoms on psychological factors or denies a patient's illness entirely, this is called Medical Gaslighting.

He labeled my symptoms as a personality disorder and belittled my status as a woman in the military. The result was that I felt hopeless and regretted my decision to share my experience.

Women's health is often overlooked and neglected, which accounts for part of the reason women are more likely to experience Medical Gaslighting.

Medical research tends to use male subjects and overlooks conditions experienced primarily by women.

A 2007 study[85] in the Journal of Women's Health found that only 24% of participants in 46 drug trials from 2004 were women. A 2011 study[86] in the same journal found that the median enrollment of women in federally funded 2009 clinical trials in nine medical journals was 37%—the same as it had been five years prior.

It should also be noted that researchers conduct five times

It wasn't that long ago when "Female Hysteria" was a common medical diagnosis. In fact, for centuries it was believed the uterus was the cause of women's hysterical symptoms. And yet, as far as we have come, we've still got a long way to go.

as many studies into erectile dysfunction as premenstrual syndrome, despite only around 19% of men suffering from erectile dysfunction while 90% of women experience symptoms of PMS.

It's not only the lack of women being included in medical research that skews the numbers. Incorrect gender biases create plenty of problems in medical care.

A 2001 study[87] published in the Journal of Law, Medicine

113

& Ethics found that many doctors believe women have a "natural capacity to endure pain" thanks to the stresses of childbirth.

A National Institute of Health study[88] also shows women are 13-25% less likely to receive opioids when they are dealing with pain.

Today, women are still more likely to have their pain described as "emotional" or "psychological," and that creates a situation where seeking proper medical care becomes stressful.

Like with Gaslighting in Emotional Abuse, those who experience it in the medical setting lose confidence in their own voice.

They also lose confidence in the medical system, feeling that all doctors will treat them with the same disregard. This leads many people to forego treatment altogether, which can lead to dire consequences.

THE BOTTOM LINE

Medical Trauma, while not commonly discussed, is trauma. It is subjective in nature, and can be compounded by Medical Gaslighting. Those who experience Medical Trauma can develop anxiety, depression, and PTSD and are at a higher risk of avoiding future (potentially necessary) medical treatments.

WORK RELATED TRAUMA

COMPASSION FATIGUE & VICARIOUS TRAUMA

Vicarious Trauma[89] is a theoretical term that focuses on the profound negative changes in a person's worldview due to the exposure to traumatic content of the people they help[90].

This is often used synonymously with Compassion Fatigue and Burnout, but some scholars argue that those terms are not quite the same. Francoise Mathieu[91], for instance, suggests that those terms are complementary, but different.

If you're reading that last paragraph and it sounded like a bunch of psychobabble, you're not wrong.

This kind of workplace-related trauma is a tricky one.

So let's start off by defining a few of those terms to get us all on the same page.

Traumatic Stress (TS) is the response to a traumatic event. It is a normal reaction to a terrible event, but symptoms usually get better over time.

Acute Stress Disorder (ASD) is the continuing and extreme traumatic stress response that significantly interferes with daily life in the month following the traumatic exposure.

Post-Traumatic Stress Disorder (PTSD) is the continuing and extreme traumatic stress response that significantly interferes with daily life for longer than a month following the traumatic exposure.

Secondary Traumatic Stress (STS) was defined by Dr. Charles Figley[92]. It is the stress resulting from helping or wanting to help a traumatized or suffering person.

Burnout (BO) Coined in the 1970s by the American psychologist Herbert Freudenberger[93]. It also describes the consequences of severe stress and high ideals in "helping" professions.

It is a syndrome resulting from chronic workplace stress that has not been successfully managed.[94]

Okay, so now we know all the other terms, let's see how Compassion Fatigue relates.

Compassion Fatigue was coined by Charles Figley in the 1980s and refers to a set of negative psychological symptoms that caregivers experience in the course of their work while being exposed to direct traumatic events or through secondary trauma.

Compassion Fatigue is an erosive process, not attributed to a single exposure to trauma. It is the result of ongoing, repeated exposure to traumatic situations, whether direct or indirect.

This places many occupations such as law enforcement, first responders, healthcare professionals, teachers, and community service workers right in the crosshairs if they have the risk factors to be affected by it.

Over time, the act of providing care in the context of human suffering and trauma wears down the individual's psychological resilience, leaving the care worker in a combined state of Burnout[95] that leads to more serious mental health conditions such PTSD, anxiety, or depression.

Essentially, the continuous exposure to the trauma of others may lead care work professionals to manifest the same or similar symptoms as the trauma survivors they have helped.

Compassion Fatigue has also been known to impact journalists and war correspondents attempting to interview refugees and others who had survived traumas. In her 2015 memoir, *Irritable Hearts: A PTSD Love Story*, human rights reporter Gabriel Mac (formerly McClelland)[96] writes about the impacts of witnessing so much suffering during an assignment in Haiti following a devastating earthquake in 2010.

- Between 40% and 85% of helping professionals develop Vicarious Trauma, Compassion Fatigue and/or high rates of traumatic symptoms, according to Compassion Fatigue expert, Francoise Mathieu[97].
- 86% of Nurses had moderate to high levels of Compassion Fatigue[98].
- 70% of Social Workers exhibited at least one symptom of Secondary Traumatic Stress[99].
- 15% of general practitioners turned to alcohol, prescription drugs or both to help them "deal with work pressures.[100]"
- 70% of Therapists (dealing with Sexual Assault survivors) experienced Vicarious Trauma[101].
- 50% of Child Protection Workers suffered from 'high' to 'very high' levels of Compassion Fatigue[102].
- 33% of Law Enforcement showed high levels of emotional exhaustion and reduced personal accomplishment; 56.1 percent scored high on the depersonalization scale[103].

- Only 15% of Law Enforcement professionals were willing to seek personal counseling as a result of Vicarious Trauma versus 59% of mental health professionals.
- Estimated prevalence rates of 11% for PTSD, 15% for depression, 15% for anxiety, and 27% for general psychological distress amongst ambulance personnel[104].

While not an exhaustive list, it definitely shows that those in the business of caring for others tend to be the most at risk of needing care themselves.

Let's look at some of the risk factors which can be associated with Compassion Fatigue:

- A personal history of trauma
- Geographical and/or social isolation
- Being overworked, overwhelmed, and/or underpaid
- Having limited professional experience and no training with Vicarious Trauma prevention
- Working with a high percentage of traumatized children
- Working with clients who are underserved and disadvantaged
- Working under stressful conditions, with limited resources

While there has been a lot of research done on identifying the prevalence and predictors of Compassion Fatigue, like workload intensity, inadequate rest time periods between shifts, task repetitiveness, low job satisfaction, poor resilience, lack of meaningful recognition, and poor managerial support.

Knowing the factors has produced little conclusive evidence to direct employers and managers in the healthcare, emergency response, and community on how to best prevent Compassion Fatigue . The focus is often on the risk factors—exposure to traumatized patients and clients in the type of work that the employees supervise and undertake.

So, at this time, the onus is primarily on the person with Compassion Fatigue to seek help whenever possible.

During a TED Talk in 2017, Patricia Smith, the founder of the Compassion Fatigue Awareness Project[105], had this to say,

"Caregivers are not good at asking for help. Asking for help is hard, no matter who you are. For nurses, doctors, teachers and more, the idea of leaving work can seem like an impossibility.

You may feel guilty or that you are abandoning your patients or students. But if you are struggling with drug or alcohol use, you need help too. Your clients, patients and students will be happy for you."

With that in mind, try to be aware of the following signs and seek immediate help:

- Experiencing lingering feelings of anger, rage, and sadness about a patient's victimization
- Becoming too emotionally involved with the patient
- Experiencing bystander guilt, shame, feelings of self-doubt
- Over-identification with the patient (having horror and rescue fantasies)
- Loss of hope, pessimism, cynicism
- Distancing, numbing, detachment, cutting patients off, or avoiding listening to a client's story of traumatic experiences

119

- Difficulty in maintaining professional boundaries with the client, such as overextending self (trying to do more than is in the role to help the patient)

TRAUMA IN MILITARY SERVICE

The U.S. has deployed troops to at least four major conflicts since 1955 (Vietnam, Gulf War, Operation Enduring Freedom, Operation Iraqi Freedom). Since September 11, 2001, alone, the U.S. military has deployed nearly 2.5 million troops to combat zones in support of the wars in Iraq and Afghanistan[106].

Trauma among military personnel continues to be an ongoing concern. Some estimate that up to 23% of post-9/11 service members have Post-Traumatic Stress Disorder[107]. Even when service personnel do not meet the full criteria for PTSD, they often have trauma symptoms and co-occurring depression, anxiety, or substance abuse.

For many service members, being away from home for long periods of time can cause problems at home or work. These problems can add to the stress.

Trauma symptoms are prevalent for National Guard and Reserve troops who deploy as well. Almost half of those who served in Operation Enduring Freedom/Operation Iraqi Freedom were Guards and Reservists[108].

Combat Service Members can be at high risk for death or injury, often work around the clock, and can experience extremely high levels of stress. Combat stress, also known as battle fatigue, is a common response to the mental and emotional strain that can result from dangerous and traumatic experiences.

120

In peacetime, active duty personnel sometimes aid in natural disaster relief and humanitarian efforts. In the service of their duty, they may be exposed to a variety of stressors and strenuous physical demands, which can result in chronic physical and mental health problems.

Women often face added difficulties during military service, especially those with young children to care for. Long deployments, sometimes with little notice, leave women feeling uncertainty and guilt about their families back home and what effect being away from their children might have.

Female service members have much higher rates of divorce and are more likely to be a single parent, and there is even a greater degree of complexity when single mothers are deployed. While the military requires a family care plan that outlines the arrangements service members have made for their children during deployments, it leaves deployed mothers open to legal notices for increases in child support, custody changes, and caregivers who can no longer continue with childcare responsibilities[109].

When returning from deployments, women can find it difficult to switch gears from Soldier to parent, which can lead to conflicts and resentment, and they may also be confronted with additional social biases.

Even today, societal norms seem to be more accepting of fathers than mothers being away from their families due to deployments[110].

Married women Veterans whose husbands are still serving on active duty must immediately begin caring for their children with little or no time to transition or readjust. Finding affordable child care may be difficult and prevent them from seeking employment, continuing their education, and seeking treatment services for mental health and adjustment problems[111,112].

For women serving in the military, Military Sexual Trauma (MST)[113] has also emerged as a significant concern. MST is defined by the VA as "experiences of Sexual Assault or repeated, threatening sexual harassment that a veteran experienced during his or her military service." National data from this program revealed that about 1 in 3 women respond "yes," that they experienced MST, when screened by their VA provider.

Recognizing stress symptoms is an important first step to recovering:

- Irritability and anger outbursts
- Excessive fear and worry
- Headaches and fatigue
- Depression and apathy
- Loss of appetite
- Problems sleeping
- Changes in behavior or personality

The Military Crisis Line
(1-800-273-8255)

The National Suicide Prevention Hotline
(1-800-273-8255)

The Veterans Crisis Line
www.veteranscrisisline.net/get-help/chat
text at 838255.

THE BOTTOM LINE

Whether male or female, being a soldier is not easy. Exposure to combat and operational stress during active duty can create lasting emotional scars. It is important to recognize the warning signs of a potential negative mental health crisis before it becomes a detriment to normal daily life.

OVERWHELMING EMOTIONAL STRAIN

Trauma exposure is the initiating factor behind PTSD, however, there could be additional influential elements to consider.

Social support, or lack of, is a critical risk factor.

Those who are limited in options for social support can be at greater risk for PTSD. After a traumatic event, the need for safe support resources is essential to help individuals process their experience in a healthy way and to regain hope through secure and safe emotional connections.

Life stressors are a risk factor as well.

When people are currently experiencing life stressors such as divorce, financial strain, work stress, or for children who are experiencing emotional challenges at school or home, the likelihood of developing PTSD can increase.

EMOTIONAL LABOR

Sociologist Arlie Hochschild[114] coined two phrases, Emotion Work, and Emotional Labor in her 1983 book, *The Managed Heart*.

The phrases were originally meant to be used as separate situational identifiers.

Emotion Work: The social tasks one performs to satisfy others. Unpaid emotional work that a person undertakes in private life.

Emotional Labor: The process of managing feelings and expressions to fulfill the emotional requirements of a job. Emotional work done in a paid work setting.

Both speak of managing personal emotions while fulfilling duties and expectations for the benefit of others. Because of the similarities in both, there are differing opinions on whether the term Emotional Labor should be used in both domestic and workplace settings.

Hochschild's study of Emotional Labor (originally only used for paid labor) echoed many of the issues around the uncompensated labor that women perform in the home. This led Hochschild to write *The Second Shift*, describing the labor performed at home in addition to the paid work performed outside of the home.

In 1975, Feminist Activist Silvia Federici[115] wrote, "Capitalist patriarchy had brainwashed women into thinking that doing dishes and diapering babies was a *natural attribute of our female physique and personality*." She made the argument for domestic duties (unpaid work), qualifying it as a form of Emotional Labor.

Sharmin Tunguz, PhD[116], an associate professor in the Department of Psychology at DePauw University, doesn't agree.

"Academically speaking, Emotional Labor is defined as the regulation of emotions for a wage. Emotional Labor is usually experienced in the service sector where jobs require employees to provide 'service with a smile.'"

Even as the scholars disagree, many women suffer under the burden both in their domestic and work lives. In her 2018 book, *Fed Up: Women, Emotional Labor, and the Way Forward*[117], Journalist Gemma Hartley firmly solidified the term Emotional Labor into our modern vocabulary.

Women are fed up because we've realized we can't clock out. We're required to work nonstop, without complaint, or asking for help. If we do, we're labeled as nags, difficult, ornery, crazy, bossy, a ball buster. Shamed into quiet compliance, Emotional Labor is expected from us no matter where we turn.

The lines have blurred so much that, in an effort to find the right term, many new ones have popped up. Mixed in with **Emotional Labor** and **Emotion Work**, we can also add **the mental load, emotional load,** and **cognitive labor**. They are all used to describe the same thing today: the often unpaid, unrecognized emotional toll of gender expectations.

No matter what you call it, managing another person's needs while meeting social expectations at the expense of one's own wellbeing, respect, and consideration is a mental drain that leads to Burnout, psychological distress, and depression.

Let's look at Emotional Labor from the two viewpoints of work and home life and how they both contribute to a negative mental state.

EMOTIONAL LABOR IN THE WORKPLACE

When thinking of Emotional Labor as it applies to the workplace, think of the phrase, "Service with a smile."

That, in essence, is what Emotional Labor in the workplace is about. The person who is being paid to serve must maintain the proper attitude at all times.

Beyond the physical or mental duties of a specific job, adopting the proper personality when dealing with others (customer, client, boss, or coworker) and accepting verbal abuse with a smile are often hidden requirements of the job.

To perform the required job appropriately means a person must either express only positive feelings, or strictly manage any of their negative feelings so as not to cause distress to others.

Masking personal feelings requires a bit of acting.

Surface acting–Faking or pretending to match the required emotional response by using rehearsed body language and responses (scripted answers — common among call centers).

You might be familiar with the term, *fake it till you make it*. That very much applies here. It is a form of Toxic Positivity.

Deep acting–Controlling and suppressing personal emotions while creating the belief that the person is actually happy, even when they are not. This is done for the customer, client, boss, or coworker's benefit to maintain a sense of positivity in the workplace.

Deep acting is looked at positively by the psychological community[118] as a method of dealing with Emotional Labor, however, many of those psychological studies praising deep acting do not account for the various moderators in the employee-work relationship.

Nor do they account for length and frequency that deep acting is required to be used as a coping mechanism[119].

Hiding or suppressing emotions for an extended period leads to high levels of stress, emotional exhaustion, internal emotional conflict, and can create disconnection for that person inhibiting close personal relationships. It's a snowball effect of mental exhaustion that leads to Burnout.

Some examples of Emotional Labor are:

- Retail workers smiling and making cheerful small talk throughout their shifts, even if they recently broke up with their partner, had a fight with their best friend, or lost their dog
- Teachers remaining calm and friendly, even as parents berate them or accuse them of neglecting their child's needs
- Flight attendants keeping up a friendly disposition in the face of demanding (and sometimes demeaning) passengers
- An Uber or Lyft driver being overly polite or chatty, especially with difficult customers, so they can maintain their star rating (If their average falls too much they can be deactivated as a driver.)
- In the corporate world, modulating emotions to maintain a calm or happy demeanor while being cut off or talked over
- Managing teams, expectations, and deadlines all while being required to walk, talk, move, and comport yourself in a ladylike way that does not come across as too abrasive or difficult for male co-workers to deal with

In an article by Eric Jaffe, The New Subtle Sexism Toward Women in the Workplace[120], he cites studies [121]that reveal there are real penalties for women who reach for success in male domains by violating perceived gender-stereotypes.

When women violate the behaviors expected of them, they're often punished.

If she's expected to be compassionate and instead acts forcefully, she's more likely to be labeled "brusque" or "uncaring" instead of "decisive."

- Women who succeed in male domains are disliked.[122]
- Women who promote themselves are less hirable.[123]
- Women who negotiate for higher pay are penalized.[124]
- Women who express anger are given lower status.[125]

Conforming to gender stereotypes isn't always beneficial for women, either.

According to one 2005 study[126] published in the Journal of Applied Psychology, when women and men behave altruistically at work, men are given accolades for doing so.

However, when women don't step up and go the extra mile, they're judged more harshly.

The impact of Emotional Labor on the people it is demanded of, is a lack of job satisfaction, high levels of stress, emotional exhaustion, internal emotional conflict, and Burnout.

COGNITIVE LABOR

(The Mental Load) outside of the workplace

According to a 2019 study[127] of nearly 400 married or partnered mothers in the U.S., nearly 65% were employed. 88% also reported they primarily managed routines at home and 76% said they were mostly responsible for maintaining regular household standards and order.

Mental load comes in different shapes and sizes, but the primary component of this is that one person is handling the majority of the work required to maintain a relationship or care for another individual while others are oblivious to the work being done and/or are unwilling to help with that work.

See how many of the following ring a bell with you:

- Always having to ask a partner for help because they are oblivious to the needs of the household without formal instruction. "Just tell me what you want me to do."
- Being required to manage the financial, medical, scheduling, and dietary needs of the household without help from anyone else
- Having to praise a partner when they complete any necessary chore toward maintaining the household despite your own work going unrecognized
- Being required to keep track of parenting-related daily details, including after-school plans, permission slips, library book due dates, or pediatrician appointments with little to no help from anyone else
- Staying on top of the kids' physical and emotional needs
- Making to-do lists, grocery lists, or chore charts (for more than just the kids)

- Being the one to purchase and wrap gifts for friends, family, children's parties, office socials, etc.
- Managing the social schedule for family, including date nights, vacations, family holidays, etc.
- Lacking the time to pursue leisure activities because any free time would impede on your partner's time to relax
- Your partner depends on you for support, but has little time to listen to your concerns

Personal Experience

I had started my business before our first child was born, and thankfully was able to work from home, which made being a mom slightly easier for me. I could adjust my schedule to our growing family's needs and still get my work done. Over the years, the amount of money I brought in ebbed and flowed, and though the amount I financially contributed to the household might not have been equal to his, the savings over having to pay for childcare more than made up for that. Still, as a working mom, I had my daily responsibilities, which more often than not meant structuring my workday around the children, leaving me working late into the evening to catch up and still having to get up at the crack of dawn for school runs. Sleep was a luxury I was never afforded, meanwhile my husband couldn't function on less than eight hours of shut-eye.

Must be nice.

On top of running my own business, being a mom meant I was the housekeeper, chef, personal shopper, chauffeur, and scheduling coordinator for the family.

The stress of trying to do it all with a less than helpful husband added up over the years until I finally hit a breaking point.

*I'm reminded of a blog post that really hit home during the two years preceding my divorce. I was in a state of emotional burnout, struggling to hold it together while wanting to keep my family from being torn apart by divorce. When I read the blog by Matthew Fray, **She Divorced Me Because I Left Dishes By The Sink** [128], I felt seen for the first time. I remember sending it to my then husband in the hopes that he might understand what I had been trying (and failing) to get him to see.*

Spoiler alert, he didn't.

Emotional labor can seem like an abstract concept, but to this day, I feel like Matthew Fray really hit the nail on the head with his raw and honest look at how emotional labor eroded what had once been a beautiful relationship. His writing is filled with poignant and hard-hitting realizations about what caused his relationship to ultimately fail.

"I always reasoned: 'If you just tell me what you want me to do, I'll gladly do it.'

But she didn't want to be my mother. She wanted to be my partner, and she wanted me to apply all of my intelligence and learning capabilities to the logistics of managing our lives and household."

The wife doesn't want to divorce her husband because he leaves used drinking glasses by the sink. She wants to divorce him because she feels like he doesn't respect or appreciate her, which suggests he doesn't love her, and she can't count on him to be her lifelong partner.

*In a follow up to that first post, **She Feels Like Your Mom And Doesn't Want To Bang You**[129], Fray continued to clarify his point, which struck right at the heart of how emotional labor works.*

"I always reasoned: 'If you just tell me what you want

me to do, I'll gladly do it.'

I wasn't asking my wife to boss me around.

I was asking my wife to HELP ME help her. Read that sentence again, guys. I wanted to help my wife. I did. But instead of actually being helpful, I put the burden of responsibility on her to manage her life, our baby's life, AND my life."

I desperately tried to get my husband to understand that his lack of ability to pick up the slack and do his part to be a 50/50 member of our relationship had put an unrepairable strain on our marriage.

I had grown to resent him over the years.

Every night he snored loudly while I paced the halls trying to console our screaming baby. Every time I saw clothes piled around, but not in the hamper. Every time I wanted to get out for some "me" time, but couldn't because he couldn't be bothered to watch his kids. Every time I had to sacrifice, because he wouldn't pull his weight in our relationship, I loved him a little less.

I know it's terrible to say, but that is how it felt. I took on all the responsibility in the household while all he had to do was get up and go to work. His day was 9-5 with weekends off, but mine was 24/7, 365.

The imbalance of our partnership was what ultimately killed it. I could no longer see in him the things that had originally attracted me to him, all I saw was another chore, another drain on my already depleted energy supply.

When I stopped caring and doing things for him, he made the same arguments as Fray outlined above. If I would only just tell him what to do, he would do it.

But I wasn't his mother, his babysitter, personal assistant, or whatever. I shouldn't have had to tell another supposedly fully-functioning adult how to be a fully-functioning adult. He could see the dirty dishes. He wasn't blind to the laundry piling up all over the floor. He was *just as capable of feeding his children as I was. But unless he was told to do it, he wouldn't.*

He was supposed to be my partner. Instead, by putting the onus on me to manage him like the other children in our household, he had become my 4th child.

And that is why I couldn't remain married to him. We didn't end because of infidelity, abuse, or any of the acceptable reasons that society deems okay to dissolve a marriage. We ended because I was drowning under the weight of all the things I was required to do as mom and wife, and I had nothing left in me to give.

And let me tell you, that is not a reason society seems to understand. It would have been 10x easier if he had cheated on me. And sometimes, I wish he had. But, even with all the flack I got from family, and all the times I was called a selfish horrible mother for breaking up our family, I would do it again.

It's not right that women are required to bear the brunt of all the emotional load while men are free to do as they please. It's not right that mothers are constantly scrutinized for every decision we make, but men get a gold star and are revered for simply showing up to their kids' soccer game.

In divorcing, my daily life didn't change much. I still have the same 24/7 365 schedule, only now I have one less person to have to manage.

His life, however, was altered drastically. Something I secretly smile about when he complains of domestic issues. Maybe if he had just tried a little harder back then, he wouldn't have it so hard now. But that ship has sailed.

If one partner constantly has to remind the other how to be an equal partner in the relationship, make to-do lists for them, or maintain a chore chart, that's work.

If you're more of a visual person, we highly recommend the comic by French cartoonist, Emma. In her comic strip, *You Should've Asked*, [130] Emma brilliantly illustrates the mental load and its effect on working mothers.

Emotional Labor is gendered, considered to be *women's work*, part of an ongoing history of care-taking labor where mostly marginalized people are expected to give their energy, time, and emotional capacity to serve others.

Women often grow up watching their own mothers managing the same expectations. Women thrive on social support, so they also tend to be around other women facing the same daily grind.

They often feel a need to wear many hats—working professional, super mom, family therapist, chef, chauffeur, financial manager, housekeeper, beauty queen, and sexual goddess.

THE BOTTOM LINE

When someone is expected to manage the emotional experiences and wellbeing of others, it is implied that the person is capable of absorbing all the negative implications that come with it. If they aren't capable, their value diminishes. This adds to the stress and anxiety of the person required to perform the Emotional Labor, and that eventually leads to Burnout.

It goes without saying that Emotional Labor tends to be exhaustive.

BURNOUT

While we are certain that you have all been nodding your heads while reading this, you're probably wondering where the trauma connection is. That is, of course, what this whole chapter is about, discussing the various types of trauma that can lead to PTSD.

That's where Burnout comes in.

The term, Burnout was coined in the 1970s by the American psychologist Herbert Freudenberger. He used it to describe the consequences of severe stress and high ideals in "helping" professions. Nowadays, the term is often used to describe the fallout or dark side of self-sacrifice. It can affect anyone, from stressed-out career-driven people to overworked employees and homemakers.

Finally recognized in 2019 by the WHO's International Classification of Diseases, after more than four decades of debate among experts, Burnout is defined as: A syndrome conceptualized as resulting from chronic workplace stress that has not been successfully managed.

It is characterized by three dimensions: 1) feelings of energy depletion or exhaustion; 2) increased mental distance from one's job, or feelings of negativism or cynicism related to one's job; and 3) reduced professional efficacy. Burnout refers specifically to phenomena in the occupational context and should not be applied to describe experiences in other areas of life.[131]

As of the writing of this book, Burnout is not listed as a diagnosis in DSM-5. It should also be noted that in the WHO's classification, Burnout is not applied to experiences in areas other than work.

So, clearly there is a lot missing from the definition. It also does not take into account the differences between men and women or the various emotional loads each is required to perform in work and/or daily life.

That said, we must understand that Burnout is much more complicated than ordinary fatigue.

Burnout is a state of emotional, physical, and mental exhaustion caused by excessive prolonged stress. Being burned out is feeling empty, mentally exhausted, and lacking motivation, with no resources left to draw on.

People experiencing Burnout often cannot see a way to change their situation. If not addressed and treated, Burnout can lead to a full-on mental health crisis.

Burnout is not caused by stress alone. Here are some of the other factors that can lead to Burnout:

- Feeling like you have little or no control over your work
- Lack of recognition or reward for good work
- Unclear or overly demanding job expectations
- Working too much, without enough time for socializing or relaxing
- Lack of close, supportive relationships
- Taking on too many responsibilities, without enough help from others
- The need to be in control
- A reluctance to delegate to others (Type A personality)
- Feeling undervalued or appreciated

Psychologists Herbert Freudenberger and Gail North have outlined the 12 phases of this stress syndrome[132]:

- **Excessive Drive/Ambition**

  Too much ambition can lead to Burnout. Ambition pushes a person to work harder.

- **Neglecting Needs**

  Begin to sacrifice self-care like sleep, exercise, and eating well.

- **Displacement of Conflict**

  Blaming the boss, the demands of the job, or colleagues for personal troubles.

- **No Time for Non-Work-Related Needs**

  Begin to withdraw from family and friends.

- **Denial**

  Impatience with others, seeing them as incompetent, lazy, or overbearing.

- **Withdrawal**

  Further pulling away from family and friends. Social invitations to parties, movies, and dinner dates start to feel burdensome.

- **Behavioral Changes**

  Those on the road to Burnout may become more aggressive and snap at loved ones for no reason.

- **Depersonalization**

  Feeling detached from life and the ability to enjoy it.

- **Inner Emptiness or Anxiety**

  Potential to turn to thrill-seeking behaviors to cope with empty feelings. Potential for substance use, gambling, or overeating.

- **Depression**

  Life loses its meaning. Extreme hopelessness.

- **Mental or Physical Collapse**

  Mental health care or medical attention may be necessary.

Ask yourself these four questions to determine if you are suffering from Burnout:

1. How often are you tired and lacking energy to go to work in the morning?
2. How often do you feel physically drained, like your batteries are dead?
3. How often is your thinking process sluggish or your concentration impaired?
4. How often do you feel emotionally detached from co-workers (or customers) and unable to be sensitive to their needs?

THE BOTTOM LINE

There is a significant association between PTSD and Burnout, particularly the depressive component. While Burnout is not currently recognized by the DSM-5, it is a serious condition that makes a person less resilient to handling additional traumas (as already described in this chapter).

TOXIC POSITIVITY

Since we're talking about social support, we cannot avoid one of the most common social support hurdles to getting help.

138

Toxic Positivity is a form of invalidation and falls into the category of Gaslighting (See Emotional Abuse).

Instead of facing difficult emotions, Toxic Positivity rejects or ignores the negative in favor of a cheerful, often falsely positive, facade.

This can come in the form of burying one's own feelings and avoiding anything negative, or it can come as a response to expressing those negative feelings with another person.

Having a positive outlook on life is good for your mental well-being. We're not denying that. However, life is not always positive. We all deal with painful emotions and experiences. Negative feelings are critical to growth. We need to experience a little negativity (or challenges) in order to live a happy life.

There's nothing wrong with looking on the bright side or trying to remain positive when times get tough, but there comes a point where denying feelings and emotions (or the feelings and emotions of others) becomes toxic.

Ignoring, invalidating, or otherwise pushing away difficult emotions, such as sadness or fear, and forcing ourselves or others to be positive can be harmful to our mental well-being and our relationships.

Practicing false cheerfulness keeps us from addressing our feelings, and the feelings of others, leaving that negativity to fester.

Toxic Positivity can cause serious harm to people who are going through difficult times. Rather than being able to share their troubles and gain much needed support, the invalidation of Toxic Positivity leaves these people feeling dismissed and ignored.

This compounds the problems they are already dealing with.

- **It's shaming**

  Toxic Positivity tells people that the emotions they are feeling are unacceptable.

- **It causes guilt**

  It sends a message that if a person can't feel positive, even in the face of tragedy, that they are doing something wrong.

- **It avoids empathy**

  Toxic Positivity allows people to sidestep emotional situations that might make them feel uncomfortable. This becomes a societal pattern. When we feel difficult emotions, we then discount, dismiss, and deny them for ourselves and others.

- **It prevents growth**

  Dismissing and denying negative feelings also prevents us from facing those challenging feelings which, if worked through, could lead to growth and deeper insight.

Common examples:

- **Feigning Gratitude**

Focusing on gratitude as a way to bypass emotions. Gratitude is not a bad thing, but it can be when you're using it to invalidate yourself.

Look on the bright side.
Count your blessings.

- **Comparing**

Just because someone else is seemingly handling a tough time "better" than you, that's no reason to start comparing. Everyone handles things in their own way.

You think you have it rough?
It could be worse.
If I can do it, so can you.

- **Dismissing Difficult Emotions**

When difficult emotions arise, you completely push them down, insisting you must stay positive. It's a form of Gaslighting.

Everything happens for a reason.
Positive Vibes Only.
Failure is not an option.
Don't worry, be happy!

A Toxic Positivity response, rather than an empathetic one, creates a disconnect in a person's ability to rely on their social support structure.

THE BOTTOM LINE

People going through trauma don't need to be told to stay positive, they need empathy. When someone is suffering, they need to know that their emotions are valid, and they can find relief and love in their friends and family.

Negative emotions need to be validated, explored, and processed.

[11] Child Maltreatment Surveillance: Uniform Definitions for Public Health and Recommended Data Elements, Version 1.0 is a set of recommendations designed to promote consistent terminology and data collection related to child maltreatment. https://www.cdc.gov/violenceprevention/pdf/CM_Surveillance-a.pdf

[12] Take The ACE Quiz — And Learn What It Does And Doesn't Mean https://www.npr.org/sections/health-shots/2015/03/02/387007941/take-the-ace-quiz-and-learn-what-it-does-and-doesnt-mean

[13] The term "betrayal blindness" was introduced by Freyd (1996), and expanded in Freyd (1999) and Freyd and Birrell (2013) in the context of Betrayal Trauma Theory. https://dynamic.uoregon.edu/jjf/institutionalbetrayal/index.html

[14] How Common is PTSD in Children and Teens? https://www.ptsd.va.gov/understand/common/common_children_teens.asp

[15] Understanding Intergenerational Trauma: An Introduction for Clinicians. January 8, 2021 Dr. Fabiana Franco, PhD, DAAETS https://www.goodtherapy.org/blog/Understanding_Intergenerational_Trauma

[16] Intergenerational Transmission of Child Abuse and Neglect: A Transdisciplinary Analysis Melissa Van Wert, PhD, Ina Anreiter, MSc, Barbara A. Fallon, PhD, and Marla B. Sokolowski, PhD https://journals.sagepub.com/doi/epub/10.1177/2470289719826101

[17] The interplay between maternal childhood maltreatment, parental coping strategies as well as endangered parenting behavior during the current SARS-cov-2 pandemic Franziska Köhler-Dauner, Vera Clemens, Katherina Hildebrand, Ute Ziegenhain, and Jörg M. Fegert https://journals.sagepub.com/doi/pdf/10.1177/25161032211014899

[18] Silva, Marta Angelica Iossi, Pereira, Beatriz, Mendonça Denisa, Nunes Berta, de Oliveira, Wanderlei Abadio. The Involvement of Girls and Boys with Bullying: An Analysis of Gender Differ-

ences. International Journal of Environmental Research and Public Health. 2013;10(12):6820–6831. Doi:10.3390/ijerph10126820 https://www.mdpi.com/1660-4601/10/12/6820/htm

[19] The School Crime Supplement (SCS) to the National Crime Victimization Survey https://nces.ed.gov/programs/coe/indicator/a10

[20] Youth Risk Behavior Surveillance System (YRBSS) https://www.cdc.gov/healthyyouth/data/yrbs/index.htm

[21] Mean Girls https://en.wikipedia.org/wiki/Mean_Girls

[22] Crossing the Line: Sexual Harassment at School https://www.aauw.org/resources/research/crossing-the-line-sexual-harassment-at-school/

[23] Sheri Madigan, PhD, Anh Ly, MA, Christina L. Rash, BA Joris Van Ouytsel, PhD,Jeff R. Temple, PhD. Prevalence of Multiple Forms of Sexting Behavior Among Youth: A Systematic Review and Meta-Analysis. JAMA Pediatr. 2018;172(4):327-335. Doi:10.1001/jamapediatrics.2017.5314 https://jamanetwork.com/journals/jamapediatrics/fullarticle/2673719

[24] New CDC Data Shows LGBTQ Youth are More Likely to be Bullied Than Straight Cisgender Youth https://www.hrc.org/news/new-cdc-data-shows-lgbtq-youth-are-more-likely-to-be-bullied-than-straight-cisgender-youth

[25] Idsoe, T., Dyregrov, A., & Idsoe, E. C. (2012). Bullying and PTSD symptoms. Journal of abnormal child psychology, 40(6), 901–911. https://doi.org/10.1007/s10802-012-9620-0

[26] Sacks, Vanessa Harbin & Murphey, David & Moore, Kristin. (2014). Adverse childhood experiences: national and state-level prevalence. 10.13140/2.1.1193.8087. https://www.researchgate.net/publication/272818291_adverse_childhood_experiences_national_and_state-level_prevalence

[27] University of Illinois at Urbana-Champaign. "Wounds from childhood bullying may persist into college years, study finds." science daily. www.sciencedaily.com/releases/2016/09/160901135546.htm

[28] Psychiatric distress and symptoms of PTSD among victims of bullying at work https://www.tandfonline.com/doi/abs/10.1080/030698804100017 23558?Src=recsys&journalcode=cbjg20&

[29] Post-traumatic stress disorder as a consequence of bullying at work and at school. A literature review and meta-analysis https://www.sciencedirect.com/science/article/pii/S1359178915000026

[30] Silvan Solomon Tomkins was a psychologist and personality theorist who developed both affect theory and script theory. Following the publication of the third volume of his book *Affect Imagery Consciousness* in 1991, his body of work received renewed interest, leading to attempts by others to summarize and popularize his theories. https://en.wikipedia.org/wiki/Silvan_Tomkins

[31] John Elliot Bradshaw was an American educator, counselor, motivational speaker, and author https://www.johnbradshaw.com/books/healing-the-shame-that-binds-you

[32] Shame vs. Guilt by Brené Brown https://brene-brown.com/blog/2013/01/14/shame-v-guilt/ and

The Power of Vulnerability TED talk by Brené Brown https://www.ted.com/talks/brene_brown_the_power_of_vulnerability?Language=en

[33] Krizan Z, & Johar O. Narcissistic rage revisited. Journal of Personality and Social Psychology. 2015;108(5):784-801. https://doi.apa.org/doilanding?Doi=10.1037%2Fpspp0000013

[34] Ava Green and Kathy Charles. "Voicing the Victims of Narcissistic Partners: A Qualitative Analysis of Responses to Narcissistic Injury and Self-Esteem Regulation." SAGE Open, (April 2019). https://doi.org/10.1177/2158244019846693.

[35] American Psychiatric Association. (2013). Diagnostic and statistical manual of mental Disorders: DSM-5-TR. Washington, D.C.: American Psychiatric Association. https://www.psychiatry.org/psychiatrists/practice/dsm

[36] Mommie Dearest, No Wire Hangers (scene). https://youtu.be/czeyyf6ppeg

Mommie Dearest (film) https://en.wikipedia.org/wiki/Mommie_Dearest_(film)

[37] Intergenerational effects of childhood maltreatment: A systematic review of the parenting practices of adult survivors of childhood abuse, neglect, and violence Carolyn A. Greene, PhD, Lauren Haisley, PhD, Cara Wallace, PsyD, and Julien D. Ford, PhD, A.B.P.P. https://doi.org/10.1016/j.cpr.2020.101891

Published: 2020-08

[38] 1999 WHO Consultation on Child Abuse Prevention. https://www.who.int/violence_injury_prevention/resources/publications/en/guidelines_chap7.pdf

[39] CDC Preventing Child Sexual Abuse facts https://www.cdc.gov/violenceprevention/childsexualabuse/fastfact.html

[40] CDC Preventing Child Sexual Abuse https://www.cdc.gov/violenceprevention/childsexualabuse/fastfact.html?CDC_AA_refval=https%3A%2F%2Fwww.cdc.gov%2Fviolenceprevention%2Fchildabuseandneglect%2Fchildsexualabuse.html

[41] Gaslight movie, released 1944. https://en.wikipedia.org/wiki/Gaslight_(1944_film)

[42] Gas Light play, written in 1938. https://en.wikipedia.org/wiki/Gas_Light

[43] The Gaslight Effect by Robin Stern, Ph.D. https://robinstern.com/

[44] The National Domestic Violence Hotline https://www.thehotline.org/resources/what-is-gaslighting/

[45] Starting in 2013, the FBI's UCR Program initiated the collection of rape data using a revised definition that removed the term "forcible" from the offense name and description. https://www.bjs.gov/arrests/templates/introduction.cfm

[46] Definition of Consent, Cornell Law School https://www.law.cornell.edu/uscode/text/10/920

[47] RAINN survivors of sexual violence: statistics
HTTPS://WWW.RAINN.ORG/STATISTICS/SURVIVORS-SEXUAL-VIOLENCE

[48] The National Intimate Partner and Sexual Violence Survey
https://www.nsvrc.org/sites/default/files/2021-04/2015data-brief508.pdf

[49] Marital Rape:New Research and Directions by Raquel Kennedy Bergen & Elizabeth Barnhill https://vawnet.org/sites/default/files/materials/files/2016-09/AR_maritalrapervised.pdf

[50] Spousal Rape - The Uncommon Law
https://www.ojp.gov/ncjrs/virtual-library/abstracts/spousal-rape-uncommon-law

[51] NCADV Domestic Violence & Sexual Assault statistics
https://ncadv.org/statistics https://assets.speakcdn.com/assets/2497/sexual_assault_dv.pdf

[52] Sexual Assault in Marriage: Prevalence, Consequences, and Treatment of Wife Rape Patricia Mahoney and Linda M. Williams http://www.ncdsv.org/images/nnfr_partnerviolence_a20-yearliteraturereviewandsynthesis.pdf

[53] Sexual Coercion and Marital Rape with Dr. Elizabeth Jeglic https://divorcesurvivalguide.libsyn.com/dsg-abuse-mini-series-sexual-coercion-and-marital-rape-with-dr-elizabeth-jeglic

[54] CDC National Intimate Partner and Sexual Violence Survey (2010) https://www.cdc.gov/violenceprevention/pdf/nisvs_report2010-a.pdf

[55] Perpetrators of Sexual Assault data from RAINN.org.
https://www.rainn.org/articles/sexual-assault

[56] National Coalition Against Domestic Violence Statistics
https://ncadv.org/statistics

[57] Lenore Edna Walker is an American psychologist who founded the Domestic Violence Institute https://www.drlenoree-walker.com/domestic-violence-institute/

[58] The Power and Control Wheel was created in 1984 by the Domestic Abuse Intervention Project (DAIP). https://www.theduluthmodel.org/wheels/

[59] National Domestic Violence Hotline 50 Obstacles to Leaving https://www.thehotline.org/resources/get-help-50-obstacles-to-leaving/

[60] New Leaf Center. Trauma Bonds: Why People Bond To Those Who Hurt Them https://newleafcenter.com/trauma-bonds-why-people-bond-to-those-who-hurt-them/

[61] Dutton DG, Painter S. Emotional attachments in abusive relationships: a test of traumatic bonding theory. Violence Vict. 1993;8(2):105-120. https://pubmed.ncbi.nlm.nih.gov/8193053/

[62] Volkow, N., Wise, R. & Baler, R. The dopamine motive system: implications for drug and food addiction. Nat Rev Neurosci 18, 741–752 (2017). https://doi.org/10.1038/nrn.2017.130

[63] Zou, Z., Song, H., Zhang, Y., & Zhang, X. (2016). Romantic Love vs. Drug Addiction May Inspire a New Treatment for Addiction. Frontiers in psychology, 7, 1436. https://doi.org/10.3389/fpsyg.2016.01436

[64] Harvard psychiatrist, Jordan Smoller https://www.psychologytoday.com/us/contributors/jordan-smoller-md

[65] The tend-and-befriend theoretical model was originally developed by Dr. Shelley E. Taylor and her research team at the University of California, Los Angeles and first described in a Psychological Review article published in the year 2000. Biobehavioral Responses to Stress in Females:Tend-and-Befriend, Not Fight-or-Flight Shelley E. Taylor, Laura Cousino Klein, Brian P. Lewis, Tara L. Gruenewald, Regan A. R. Gurung, and John A. Updegraff. University of California, Los Angeles https://scholar.harvard.edu/marianabockarova/files/tend-and-befriend.pdf

[66] Biobehavioral Responses to Stress in Females:Tend-and-Befriend, Not Fight-or-Flight Shelley E. Taylor, Laura Cousino Klein, Brian P. Lewis, Tara L. Gruenewald, Regan A. R. Gurung, and John A. Updegraff. University of California, Los Angeles https://scholar.harvard.edu/marianabockarova/files/tend-and-befriend.pdf

[67] Operant Conditioning Behavior, B.F. Skinner https://www.bfskinner.org/

[68] Jacqueline C. Campbell PhD, RN, Daniel Webster ScD, MPH, Jane Koziol-mclain, PhD, RN, et al. Risk Factors for Femicide in Abusive Relationships: Results From a Multisite Case Control Study. Am J Public Health. 2003;93(7):1089-1097. Doi:10.2105/ajph.93.7.1089

[69] Dutton DG, Painter S. Emotional attachments in abusive relationships: a test of traumatic bonding theory. Violence Vict. 1993;8(2):105-120. https://pubmed.ncbi.nlm.nih.gov/8193053/

[70] Van Wert M, Anreiter I, Fallon BA, Sokolowski MB. Intergenerational transmission of child abuse and neglect: a transdisciplinary analysis. Gender and the Genome. 2019;3:247028971982610. Doi:10.1177/2470289719826101 https://genderandthegenome.org/

[71] Nursing practice: The Ethical Issues Andrew Jameton - 1984 - repository.library.georgetown.edu https://repository.library.georgetown.edu/handle/10822/800986

[72] Shay, J. (2014). Moral injury. Psychoanalytic Psychology, 31(2), 182–191. https://doi.org/10.1037/a0036090

[73] Moral injury and moral repair in war veterans: A preliminary model and intervention strategy. Litz, et al. https://www.sciencedirect.com/science/article/abs/pii/S0272735809000920?Via%3Dihub

[74] Williamson, V., Stevelink, S., & Greenberg, N. (2018). Occupational moral injury and mental health: Systematic review and meta-analysis. The British Journal of Psychiatry, 212(6), 339-346. Doi:10.1192/bjp.2018.55 https://www.cambridge.org/core/services/aop-cambridge-core/content/view/5DC1F4B8FFF97DA27940940FE87CB527/s0007125018000557a.pdf/occupational-moral-injury-and-mental-health-systematic-review-and-meta-analysis.pdf

[75] Beyond PTSD: Soldiers Have Injured Souls by Diane Silver, Miller-Mccune https://truthout.org/articles/beyond-ptsd-soldiers-have-injured-souls/

[76] Moral injury and moral repair in war veterans: A preliminary model and intervention strategy. Litz, et al. https://www.sciencedirect.com/science/article/abs/pii/S0272735809000920?Via%3Dihub

[77] Listening to Shame Brené Brown TED Talk https://www.ted.com/talks/brene_brown_listening_to_shame?Language=en

[78] "Institutional Betrayal" as connected with betrayal trauma theory was introduced in presentations by Freyd in early 2008 , Platt, Barton, & Freyd (2009) , and in a 2013 research report (Smith & Freyd, 2013). Institutional betrayal is a core focus of the book *Blind to Betrayal*, by Freyd and Birrell, 2013. The current and most definitive exploration of institutional betrayal is presented in the *American Psychologist* (Smith & Freyd, 2014). Also see Platt, M., Barton, J., & Freyd, J.J. (2009). A Betrayal Trauma Perspective on Domestic Violence. https://dynamic.uoregon.edu/jjf/articles/pbf09.pdf

[79] What is DARVO? Jennifer J. Freyd, PhD https://dynamic.uoregon.edu/jjf/definedarvo.html

[80] South Park It's Called DARVO https://southpark.cc.com/video-clips/gfwbrf/south-park-it-s-called-darvo

[81] What is a doula? https://www.dona.org/what-is-a-doula/

[82] Effect of Immediate vs Delayed Pushing on Rates of Spontaneous Vaginal Delivery Among Nulliparous Women Receiving Neuraxial Analgesia A Randomized Clinical Trial https://jamanetwork.com/journals/jama/fullarticle/2706136

[84] When Treatment Becomes Trauma: Defining, Preventing, and Transforming Medical Trauma https://www.counseling.org/docs/default-source/vistas/when-treatment-becomes-trauma-defining-preventing-.pdf

[85] Adherence to Federal Guidelines for Reporting of Sex and Race/Ethnicity in Clinical Trials https://www.liebertpub.com/doi/epdf/10.1089/jwh.2006.15.1123

[86] Inclusion, Analysis, and Reporting of Sex and Race/Ethnicity in Clinical Trials: Have We Made Progress? https://www.ncbi.nlm.nih.gov/pmc/articles/PMC3058895/

[87] The Girl Who Cried Pain: A Bias Against Women in the Treatment of Pain https://papers.ssrn.com/sol3/papers.cfm?Abstract_id=383803

[88] Gender Disparity in Analgesic Treatment of Emergency Department Patients with Acute Abdominal Pain https://onlinelibrary.wiley.com/doi/full/10.1111/j.1553-2712.2008.00100.x

[89] Vicarious Trauma Fact Sheet American Counseling Association https://www.counseling.org/docs/trauma-disaster/fact-sheet-9---vicarious-trauma.pdf

[90] Transforming the Pain: A Workbook on Vicarious Traumatization (Norton Professional Books (Paperback)) by Karen W. Saakvitne and Laurie Anne Pearlman | Oct 17, 1996 https://www.amazon.com/Transforming-Pain-Vicarious-Traumatization-Professional/dp/0393702332

[91] Mathieu, F. (2012). The Compassion Fatigue Workbook: Creative Tools for Transforming Compassion Fatigue and Vicarious Traumatization (1st ed.). Routledge. https://doi.org/10.4324/9780203803349

[92] Figley,Charles R. (Ed.). (1995). Compassion fatigue: Coping with secondary traumatic stress disorder in those who treat the traumatized. Brunner/Mazel. https://psycnet.apa.org/record/1995-97891-000

[93] Staff Burn-Out by Herbert J. Freudenberger First published: Winter 1974 https://doi.org/10.1111/j.1540-4560.1974.tb00706.x

[94] ICD-11 for Mortality and Morbidity Statistics - QD85 Burnout https://icd.who.int/browse11/l-m/en#/http://id.who.int/icd/entity/129180281

[95] Compassion Fatigue among Healthcare, Emergency and Community Service Workers: A Systematic Review https://www.ncbi.nlm.nih.gov/pmc/articles/PMC4924075/

[96] Gabriel Mac, award-winning journalist and author http://gabrielmac.com/

[97] Mathieu, F. (2012). The Compassion Fatigue Workbook: Creative Tools for Transforming Compassion Fatigue and Vicarious Traumatization (1st ed.).

150

Routledge. https://doi.org/10.4324/9780203803349

[98] Rajeswari, H., Sreelekha, B., Nappinai, S., Subrahmanyam, U., & Rajeswari, V. (2020). Impact of accelerated recovery program on compassion fatigue among nurses in South India. Iranian Journal of Nursing and Midwifery Research, 25(3), 249–253. Doi:10.4103/ijnmr.ijnmr_218_19 Retrieved from https://www.ncbi.nlm.nih.gov/pmc/articles/PMC7299415/

[99] Bride, B. E. (2007). Prevalence of secondary traumatic stress among social workers. Social Work, 52(1), 63–70. Retrieved from https://academic.oup.com/sw/article-abstract/52/1/63/1943661?Redirectedfrom=fulltext

[100] Dumitrascu, C.I., Mannes, P., Gamble, L., Selzer, J. (2014, January). Substance Use Among Physicians and Medical Students. Retrieved from http://msrj.chm.msu.edu/wp-content/uploads/2014/04/MSRJ-Winter-2014-Substance-Use-Among-Physicians-and-Medical-Students.pdf

[101] Lobel,The vicarious effects of treating female rape survivors: The therapist's perspective. (doctoraldissertation, University of Pennsylvania, 1997). Dissertation Abstracts International: Section B: The Sciences and Engineering, Vol 57(11-B), May 1997. Pp. 7230.

[102] Conrad, D., & Kellar-Guenther, Y. (2006). Compassion fatigue, burnout, and compassion satisfaction among Colorado child protection workers. Child Abuse and Neglect, 30(10), 1071-1080.

[103] Hawkins, H.C. (2001). Police officer burnout: A partial replication of Maslach's burnout inventory. Police Quarterly, 4(3), 343-360.

[104] Petrie, K., Milligan-Saville, J., Gayed, A., Deady, M., Phelps, A., Dell, L., Forbes, D., Bryant R. A., Calvo R. A., Glozier, N., Harvey, S.B. Prevalence of PTSD and common mental disorders amongst ambulance personnel: a systematic review and meta-analysis. Soc Psychiatry Epidemiol. 2018 Sep;53(9):897-909. Doi: 10.1007/s00127-018-1539-5. Epub 2018 Jun 5. PMID: 29869691.

[105] Patricia Smith, the founder of the Compassion Fatigue Awareness project https://www.youtube.com/watch?V=7keppa8xras

[106] Institute of Medicine (US) Committee on the Initial Assessment of Readjustment Needs of Military Personnel, Veterans, and Their Families. Returning Home from Iraq and Afghanistan: Preliminary Assessment of Readjustment Needs of Veterans, Service Members, and Their Families. Washington (DC): National Academies Press (US); 2010. 2, Operation Enduring Freedom and Operation Iraqi Freedom: demographics and impact. Available from: https://www.ncbi.nlm.nih.gov/books/NBK220068/

[107] Meyer, E. C., La Bash, H., debeer, B. B., Kimbrel, N. A., Gulliver, S. B., & Morissette, S. B. (2019). Psychological inflexibility predicts PTSD symptom severity in war veterans after accounting for established PTSD risk factors and personality. Psychological Trauma: Theory, Research, Practice, and Policy, 11, 383–390. https://doi.org/10.1037/tra0000358

[108] Sadeh, N., Lusk, J., & Marx, B. P. (2017). Military trauma. In S. N. Gold (Ed.), APA handbook of trauma psychology: Foundations in knowledge (pp. 133–144). American Psychological Association. https://doi.org/10.1037/0000019-008

[109] Abigail H. Gewirtz, PhD, Barbara J. Mcmorris, PhD, Sheila Hanson, PhD, and Laurel Davis, M.A. Family adjustment of deployed and non-deployed mothers in families with a parent deployed to Iraq or Afghanistan. Prof Psychol Res Pr. 2014 Dec;45(6):465-477. Doi: 10.1037/a0036235. PMID: 25663739; PMCID: PMC4315359. https://www.ncbi.nlm.nih.gov/pmc/articles/PMC4315359/

[110] Shamed for their sacrifice: Military moms don't always get a hero's welcome home https://www.today.com/parents/military-moms-are-getting-shamed-when-they-deploy-t141710

[111] Women Veterans: The Long Journey Home https://www.dav.org/wp-content/uploads/women-veterans-study.pdf

[112] America's Women Veterans: Military Service History and VA Benefit Utilization Statistics https://www.va.gov/vetdata/docs/specialreports/final_womens_report_3_2_12_v_7.pdf

[113] Military Sexual Trauma fact sheet https://www.mentalhealth.va.gov/docs/mst_general_factsheet.pdf

[114] Arlie Hochschild - https://sociology.berkeley.edu/professor-emeritus/arlie-r-hochschild

[115] Wages against Housework by Silvia Federici https://caringla-bor.files.wordpress.com/2010/11/federici-wages-against-house-work.pdf

[116] Sharmin Tunguz, PhD - https://www.depauw.edu/academ-ics/college-of-liberal-arts/psychology/faculty-staff/de-tail/1716296280678/

[117] Gemma Hartley's Fed Up: Emotional Labor, Women, and the Way Forward http://www.gemmahartley.com/

[118] Are coworkers getting into the act? An examination of emotion regulation in coworker exchanges. https://psycnet.apa.org/rec-ord/2019-71495-001

[119] Daily Emotional Labor, Negative Affect State, and Emotional Exhaustion: Cross-Level Moderators of Affective Commitment Retrieved from: https://www.mdpi.com/2071-1050/10/6/1967

[120] The New Subtle Sexism Toward Women in the Workplace by Erik Jaffe https://www.fastcompany.com/3031101/the-new-sub-tle-sexism-toward-women-in-the-workplace

[121] Heilman, Madeline E, and Tyler G Okimoto. "Why are women penalized for success at male tasks?: the implied communality deficit." *The Journal of applied psychology* vol. 92,1 (2007): 81-92. doi:10.1037/0021-9010.92.1.81 https://pub-med.ncbi.nlm.nih.gov/17227153/

[122] Heilman, M. E., & Okimoto, T. G. (2007). Why are women pe-nalized for success at male tasks?: the implied communality defi-cit. *The Journal of applied psychology, 92*(1), 81–92. https://doi.apa.org/doiLanding?doi=10.1037%2F0021-9010.92.1.81

[123] Moss-Racusin, C.A., & Rudman, L.A. (2010). Disruptions in Women's Self-Promotion: The Backlash Avoidance Model 1. Psy-chology of Women Quarterly, 34, 186 - 202. https://jour-nals.sagepub.com/doi/10.1111/j.1471-6402.2010.01561.x

[124] Hannah Riley Bowles, Linda Babcock, Lei Lai, (2007). Social incentives for gender differences in the propensity to initiate ne-

gotiations. Organizational Behavior and Human Decision Processes Volume 103, Issue 1, May 2007, Pages 84-103. https://doi.org/10.1016/j.obhdp.2006.09.001

[125] Brescoll, V. L., & Uhlmann, E. L. (2008). Can an Angry Woman Get Ahead? Status Conferral, Gender, and Expression of Emotion in the Workplace. Psychological science, 19(3), 268–275. https://doi.org/10.1111/j.1467-9280.2008.02079.x

[126] Heilman, M. E., & Chen, J. J. (2005). Same Behavior, Different Consequences: Reactions to Men's and Women's Altruistic Citizenship Behavior. Journal of Applied Psychology, 90(3), 431–441. https://doi.org/10.1037/0021-9010.90.3.

[127] Ciciolla, Lucia & Luthar, Suniya. (2019). Invisible Household Labor and Ramifications for Adjustment: Mothers as Captains of Households. Sex Roles. 81. 1-20. 10.1007/s11199-018-1001-x.

[128] She Divorced Me Because I Left Dishes By The Sink – Matthew Fray https://mustbethistalltoride.com/2016/01/14/she-divorced-me-because-i-left-dishes-by-the-sink/

[129] She Feels Like Your Mom and Doesn't Want to Bang You https://matthewfray.com/2016/02/10/she-feels-like-your-mom-and-doesnt-want-to-bang-you/

[130] You Should've Asked by Emma https://www.workingmother.com/this-comic-perfectly-explains-mental-load-working-mothers-bear

https://english.emmaclit.com/

[131] ICD-11 for Mortality and Morbidity Statistics - QD85 Burnout https://icd.who.int/browse11/l-m/en#/http://id.who.int/icd/entity/129180281

[132] Kaschka, W.P., Korczak, D., & Broich, K. Burnout: a Fashionable Diagnosis https://www.ncbi.nlm.nih.gov/pmc/articles/PMC3230825/#R8

CHAPTER 4 PTSD: DOWN AND DIRTY FACTS

Not everyone who is exposed to trauma or traumatic events will develop symptoms of PTSD, but the possibility is there. That's where the criteria come into play. There are five major criteria to PTSD that we need to know about, because they are what our therapist will use to diagnose our PTSD.

> **Criteria** are the standards on which a diagnosis is decided. **Criteria** is plural; **criterion** is singular.

CRITERION A: DEFINITION

This criterion gives us the DSM's definition of trauma: "actual or threatened exposure to death, serious injury, or sexual violence." This is a big umbrella; there are many life events that could fit under it. Chapter 3 outlined many of the traumas that fall under this umbrella.

As you're probably already noticing, trauma is a ubiquitous experience, especially for women. The data are clear: most of us have either experienced trauma ourselves or we know someone who has.

Let's talk about the term *"actual or threatened exposure."* We all have a physical and psychological reaction to threats: fight, flight, freeze (*freeze* is the red-headed stepchild of trauma, and more on that later), or tend-and-befriend (more common among women).

We discussed this in an earlier chapter (See: How Trauma is Defined). Studies have shown that men and women cope with stress differently. Because women are biologically wired towards protecting and nurturing, they often respond to stress by trying to calm and seek or create support.

In simple terms, tend-and-befriend is a response aimed at diffusing a situation to avoid further problems. It does not, however, negate the current trauma being experienced by that person.

Our body and brain will react the same whether the threat is *actual* or *threatened*.

Our brain's #1 job is to keep us alive. When there is a perceived threat, our hearts beat faster to get more blood to our muscles, our eyes dilate, and we sweat or shake. This is our brain preparing us to do what we need to in order to stay alive.

Easy day. Now that we know what trauma is, we go to...

CRITERION B: INTRUSION SYMPTOMS

Let's say an intruder breaks into our home. They break in when we're not ready or expecting it and they try to take all our stuff. That's what intrusion symptoms feel like.

We're going to go through these five intrusion symptoms and translate again from clinician-to-English so that we've got this.

> **Intrusion Symptom 1** *as written*: "Recurrent, involuntary, and intrusive distressing memories of the traumatic event(s)."
>
> **Translation**: "We can't stop thinking about it."

Intruders come into our house when we don't want them and we have zero control over them. This is what intrusive memories do; they break into our mind when we don't want them to, they do what they want, and it happens a lot (our brain is in a bad neighborhood).

> **Intrusion Symptom 2** *as written*: "Recurrent distressing dreams in which the content and/or affect of the dream are related to the traumatic event(s)."
>
> **Translation**: "Nightmares... weird dreams that can feel scary."

Recurrent means that they happen over and over, and distressing means that they're stressful.

On TV, when someone has a nightmare or a flashback, they relive the trauma happening again exactly the way it did originally in real life, but nightmares can be uniquely terrifying in ways all their own.

They can have elements of our trauma, elements of our fears, and other powerful emotions.

> **Intrusion Symptom 3** *as written*: "Disso-ciative reactions (e.g. flashbacks) in which the individual feels or acts as if the trau-matic event(s) were occurring."
>
> **Translation**: "Strange feelings/experiences that remind us of the trauma, mess with our head, and make us feel crazy."

Dissociation is a 50-cent word that means *disconnection*, and PTSD can definitely make us feel disconnected from ourselves. Sometimes, this looks like intense emotions that come out of nowhere, and we feel sad or anxious "for no reason." Sometimes, it feels like everything around us isn't real or is "off" and we can't really explain it.

Sometimes, it looks more like confusion. Unfortunately, this is normal for PTSD.

Since this topic is already uncomfortable, let's go a little deeper in the water: *hallucinations*. This is when we see, hear, smell, taste, or feel something we objectively know is not there.

Like when we smell something burning (and we know there's no fire) or we hear gunshots, or think we see peo-ple following us.

From a clinician viewpoint, we want to be straight with you:

We have never seen a case of PTSD without hallucinations.

Never. And we need to talk about this openly because hallucinations make us feel legit crazy in a way that other symptoms don't. Ditto for flashbacks.

What's a Flashback?

Like nightmares, flashbacks are nothing like what we see in the movies. Flashbacks can feel like walking, talking nightmares; they are intense episodes that happen while we're fully awake. Flashbacks strike suddenly and feel uncontrollable. They are more like a nightmare than a memory because sometimes we can't tell the difference between a flashback and reality. They're vivid and feel unbelievably real. Unlike a movie clip, in flashbacks, we can vividly see, hear, taste, and smell things. It's terrifying because it feels like the trauma is happening all over again. Those of us who experience flashbacks often feel like we're going insane. We're not; this is a known PTSD symptom.

When we don't know that hallucinations and flashbacks are an expected part of PTSD, we can feel like we're going crazy and have no way of stopping the visions from haunting us. This leads many to seriously consider suicide.

When experiencing recurring hallucinations and flashbacks, we stop trusting our brain and body. We become frightened of ourselves and our reactions.

We ask ourselves, *"What if I hurt my family?"* or *"What if I lose it in the middle of Walmart?"*

When we look at this logically, suicide makes a lot of sense (but it isn't the answer). We very much get you; it can feel like we'll never come back from this. **But we can.**

For now, let this sink in:

Hallucinations and flashbacks are a normal part of PTSD.

Normal doesn't mean that it's okay. It just means that hallucinations and flashbacks are common and not unexpected. This is par for the course; **you are not a freak.**

> **4 & 5 as written:** "Intense or prolonged psychological distress (symptom 4) or physical distress (symptom 5) to internal or external cues."
>
> **Translation:** "Triggers mess with our physical bodies and our minds."

Symptoms 4 and 5 are two sides of the same coin, so we'll group them together:

We all have physical and psychological reactions to threats. This means that our bodies and our brains react. *Cues* are better described as **triggers**:

Triggers: stimuli that cause our bodies and brains to react.

Triggers can be internal (like pain) or external (like the sound of a car backfiring). They can bring us right back to our trauma. The smell of our attacker's cologne, a box in the middle of the road, the sound of a gunshot - these are all examples of potential triggers.

Triggers can make our hearts race to having a full-blown panic attack.

160

Unfortunately, we don't know our triggers until we experience them. It's the worst kind of surprise.

FOOT STOMP

For criterion B, the DSM-5 states that we must have one or more of these symptoms. So, if we meet one out of five, or we won the PTSD lottery and have them all, we meet this criterion. This is a common clinical error; we do not have to have all five symptoms to meet this criterion.

CRITERION C: AVOIDANCE SYMPTOMS

The DSM defines this as avoiding *internal things* (like memories, thoughts, or feelings) or avoiding *external things* (like people, places, and things that remind us of the trauma).

Those of us with PTSD will go way out of our way to avoid anything that reminds us of our trauma.

Thank you Captain Obvious!

This makes a lot of sense: **why *wouldn't* we want to dodge memories and reactions that make us feel crazy?** This is why drug and alcohol disorders are common with PTSD. Numbing the pain is easier.

Friends, we'll go way, way out of our way to avoid anything that reminds us of our trauma.

While this may seem downright insane to other people, it makes total sense in the context of PTSD.

Common examples are:

- Stop watching the news or using social media because of stories or posts that remind us of a trauma
- Go out of our way to stay away from the scene of our attack or places that remind us of the assault
- Running errands at odd hours to avoid crowds
- Arriving early so we can choose a seat away from the window

Avoidance can get complex; we will go to extremes to avoid potential triggers.

Our brain's job is (1) to keep us alive, and (2) to understand meaning. Avoidance is incredibly logical in this context, so be easy on yourself.

CRITERION D: "NEGATIVE ALTERATION IN COGNITION AND MOOD."

This means "negative changes in our thoughts and feelings." There are seven of these symptoms, and we need *two out of seven* to meet this criterion. Let's go through them:

Symptom 1: We can't remember important parts of the trauma.

When our bodies are in fight, flight, or freeze response, our brains shift everything to survival.

It's not unusual for folks with PTSD to forget or not remember significant aspects of the trauma until a trigger strikes.

162

Symptom 2: Persistent and exaggerated negative beliefs about ourselves, other people, and the world.

In Cognitive Processing Therapy, we call these "stuck points," and they definitely get us stuck. We start to believe extreme thoughts, like:

No one can be trusted.

I'll never get better.

This world is a screwed-up place.

Symptom 3: Persistent and distorted thoughts about what caused the trauma or what happened because of the trauma.

These thoughts lead us to blame ourselves or others. Self-blame is common, even when we know our thoughts are not logical. These are thoughts like:

If I had told someone, the abuse would have stopped.

I should have known that walking home alone was unsafe.

If I didn't freeze, I could have done something differently.

These distorted thoughts feel 100% convincing, but we need to ask ourselves if it's possible that we're wrong. We don't have to decide one way or the other, but we need to ask if it's *possible*. The reason we need to talk about this is that these thoughts make us want to commit suicide. More on this later, but for now, let's leave this here:

If it's possible that we're wrong, then it's possible killing ourselves isn't the right answer.

TRUTH BOMB: LET'S TALK ABOUT FREEZING

We hear about fight or flight all the time, but freeze is the red-headed stepchild of trauma. All three, fight, flight, _and_ freeze, are all normal neuro-biological responses to fear, but, if we don't know this, we can feel guilty, angry, or like we "let it happen" when our body freezes in the face of trauma.

First, let's address the fantasy that we have a choice whether our body goes into fight, flight, or freeze, because that's not a thing. When we're in danger, our brain kicks into high gear and takes over to protect our life. We do not get a choice; in a split second our brain makes the choice for us.

Think about those nature shows where lions are hunting gazelle-snacks. Flight or freeze are legit survival methods.

Symptom 4: Persistent negative emotional state (e.g., fear, horror, anger, guilt, or shame).

We feel crappy - a lot.

Symptom 5: Diminished interest or participation in significant activities.

Relaxing and having fun can feel like a colossal waste of time. It's easier to stay at home. Even things we used to enjoy don't meet the muster anymore: going out with friends, relaxing, reading, or taking a bath.

This can affect our family, too, because we're not spending as much time with them.

We only have so much bandwidth, friend.

When our mind is busy combatting all those intrusion symptoms and avoiding things, it's hard to concentrate on anything else, especially relaxing or having fun.

Symptom 6: Feeling detached or estranged from others.

Feeling disconnected and alienated from other people is common.

Symptom 7: Persistent inability to feel positive emotions.

This one is going to hurt - but if we can't talk about it here, where can we?

Let's think of emotions as a continuum: on one side we have all our bad emotions that we don't want to feel, like sadness, guilt, or loss.

In the middle are medium feelings like "meh," ambivalence, or not caring, and on the other end are good emotions we want to feel, like happiness, joy, and laughter. It looks like this:

FEELINGS I DON'T WANT TO FEEL   FEELINGS I DO WANT TO FEEL

SADNESS, FEAR, GUILT   RAGE, ANGER   SARCASM, "MEH," WHO CARES?   INTEREST, FASCINATION, WONDER   LOVE, JOY

Remember criterion C, avoidance? That's when we go way out of our way to avoid anything that reminds us of our trauma. This includes all the stuff we don't want to feel, like regret and sorrow. It makes sense that we want to avoid feeling crappy, and the hope is that we can avoid feeling crappy and enjoy the right side of the scale only. That makes sense, but feelings don't work that way.

See, things on this feelings continuum attenuate from both ends in equal measure. This means that when we avoid those crappy feelings on the left, we become *unable* to feel the good feelings we want on the right. It's a completely unexpected second-order effect, but that's how the brain works. We avoid the feelings on the left and the feelings from the right reduce in equal measure until our continuum looks like this:

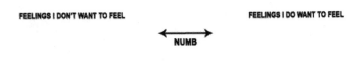

> *We've worked to avoid the things we don't want to feel, but now we literally cannot feel joy, laughter, or happiness.*

We end up in this horrible place called "numb" and it feels frightening.

Our spouse will come up to us and want to discuss something deeply upsetting - and we know they have every right to be upset - but we feel nothing.

Our friends will try to talk to us about how we've been acting, and we can see they are worried about us, but it feels like we're outside of ourselves watching this whole interaction.

Our kids come up to us crying, and we don't feel anything. Maybe we even think, "quit your crying, you big baby." *What the hell? Did I just really think that?*

> *We feel nothing, and we know we should feel something.*

We can ask ourselves, *"what is wrong with me? What kind of monster feels nothing?"* or think, *"Maybe I really am an animal."* We google our questions to see if we're a psychopath. (Calm down; you're not a psychopath.)

After feeling numb for a while, we get an idea: *I'll kill myself.* Suddenly, unexpectedly, we feel *something*. It's not joy, but it's not numb. In fact, it's the first time we've felt something outside of numb for a while - the closest we've been to feeling happy in a long time. Not because suicide ever fixes things the way we think it will, but because we have an answer when we didn't have one before. Any feelings at this point are amazing. It's at this point that we tell ourselves the lie,

"This must be the best way - because why would I feel this way if it wasn't?"

This is amplified by outside validation from people who care about us—our spouse, colleagues, and friends. They say, *"It's good to see you smiling again! You look like you're doing better today!"*

They are happy to see us feeling something again. We are happy to be feeling anything at all, and it is all because of the lie. That only reinforces it in our minds. We think it has to be the solution.

Fast forward: it's not.

FEELINGS ARE NOT FACTS.

We're going to have some real talk about suicide in a future chapter because no one talks about it and we need to. We're not trying to read you.

We've experienced this and heard this echoed thousands of times with clients.

If you're feeling this way right now, put this book down and read **Suicide: The Forever Decision** by Paul G. Quinnett, PhD. It's available in several places to download the PDF for free. Dr. Quinnett is brilliant, and we highly recommend it.

> **Remember:** We only need 2/7 symptoms to meet this criterion.

We know this is exhausting. Last one:

CRITERION E: SIGNIFICANT CHANGES IN AROUSAL OR REACTIVITY ASSOCIATED WITH THE TRAUMA

This kind of arousal doesn't have to do with sex. In this case, arousal means that your brain and your body are alert, awake, and ready. This makes sense because:

If our brain doesn't feel safe, it will keep us on high alert so we don't get hurt

Pure logic from our brain's perspective, but this doesn't work well in everyday life. Like criterion D, **this requires two symptoms**, not all of them.

Symptom 1: Irritable Behavior or Angry Outbursts (with little or no provocation) - can be verbal or physical

You've been through some stuff. This happens.

Symptom 2: Reckless or Self-Destructive Behavior

High-risk behavior on PTSD is a different animal. Think of driving your motorcycle without a helmet, while high, to pick up your daughter from daycare (true case). Think back to avoidance, too - we destroy our good marriages, eviscerate our best friends, and show up piss drunk to family reunions. Total self-destruction - now you know why.

Symptom 3: Hyper-vigilance

This is heightened alertness and behavior aimed at keeping us safe. We stay on guard, even when we logically know we're okay. Our brain and body stay alert and ready for fight, flight, or freeze. It's exhausting to maintain this for a prolonged period, and we can't relax.

Symptom 4: Exaggerated Startle Response

Being startled (shocked, surprised) is an unconscious defensive response to sudden noises or perceived threats. We always feel on edge.

Symptom 5: Problems with Concentration

We only have so much bandwidth, so when our mind is busy with intrusion symptoms and avoidance, it's hard to concentrate on anything else.

Symptom 6: Problems Sleeping

These can be problems falling asleep, staying asleep, or experiencing restless sleep.

> **Remember:** We only need 2/6 symptoms to meet this criterion.

We'll cover the last three criteria in brief because they are not complicated.

Criterion F says that these symptoms have been around for over one month.

Criterion G wants to ensure that these symptoms are problematic and are affecting our everyday real life.

Criterion H reminds us that if these symptoms are the result of a substance (like a medication) or a physical illness, then it's not PTSD.

CHAPTER 5 HOW CHANGE HAPPENS

AN INTRODUCTION TO THE "BIG TWO"

TRIGGER WARNING: a lot of you are not going to like what we're about to say (#meanladies). But to recover from PTSD or Moral Injury, we need to start with an honest conversation about our fundamental belief systems. That means honestly asking ourselves the tough questions.

> 1. Do I believe change is possible?
> 2. Do I want to change?

These are the Big Two. And as brutal as they are, we must answer them honestly before we start our healing journey.

- If we do not believe change is possible, we're right.
- If we don't want to change, we're wasting our time.

This is a hard truth. The goal of this book is to help you heal, but you have to be willing.

We realize that those questions are not easy to answer. You may be yelling back at us right now,

"You don't understand what I've done, where I've been, how it happened - you don't get it."

You're right; we haven't walked your walk. What we're asking you to do is have a brutally honest talk with yourself and ask,

> *"Do I believe that change is possible for me?"*

> **The reason we ask the Big Two questions is because no therapist, no research - no one and no thing outside of ourselves - can convince us something is true when we very fundamentally believe it is not.**

Read that text box again.

Q1

> *"Do I believe that it is possible that I can recover from my PTSD symptoms and reclaim my life?"*

We know that's what we want, but this is a different question. We must ask, "do I believe that this is possible *for me*?"

We can expand on this:

- Is it possible that I could get to a point where I'm not thinking about this every single day?
- Do I believe that it's possible for me not to feel suicidal anymore?
- Is it possible that I'm a fundamentally good person and that this PTSD is tricking me into believing I'm not?
- Is it possible that I can learn to understand myself and maybe even forgive myself?
- Do I believe any of this is even possible?

Q2

This one is a bit harder.

"Do I want to change?"

Treatment for PTSD is going to create a lot of change. If we want to reclaim our life, we have to be willing to accept that recovery takes work. Are we willing to do the work that it's going to take? Do we want it badly enough to get out of our comfort zone, to do the difficult thing, if that is what it will take to get better?

> Choosing to go through PTSD treatment involves risk, since successful PTSD treatment requires working with another person—a licensed treatment professional. We have to choose to be our authentic and raw selves with them.

There is no denying that treatment is hard work. Being vulnerable and exposing our truth to another person is frightening. We may feel fear of judgment or reliving the trauma, and that is the fear that has probably kept you in place, suffering with PTSD. Change is frightening, but the rewards are worth the risk. However, only you can decide if you are willing to try.

PTSD treatment affects our lives and our relationships with ourselves and others.

Not everyone is comfortable being wrong, and we may discover in treatment that we have been unfair to ourselves or made assumptions that were not correct. We may need to make amends, or we may need to forgive.

Not everyone who struggles with PTSD believes change is possible. Not everyone wants to change. *And that is okay.* Zero judgement here. We get it.

Maybe you're a spouse or a friend reading this book because you want to help someone you care about, and the idea of your loved one not getting help is not okay with you.

Here's the thing: Yes, it is okay, and we recommend you stand down for your own sanity. This is hard to hear, so we're saying this with love: *you have no control over what someone else believes.* You can't make someone else want to change because that is not how life works. We know this feels unfair because you see how this is affecting your loved one—and you—and we realize this may be tearing you and your family apart.

> *The fact is that the only person who can change me is me, and the only person who can change you is you.*

Are we asking you to give up hope? Absolutely not. We're asking you to recognize that **people get help when they are ready, not when we are ready**. And that's okay.

> **There are many of us reading this who are on the fence about the Big Two questions, and that is okay, too.**

It is 100% okay not to feel all-in.

Instead, we'll ask you this: *Is it possible that you are stronger than you think?*

Trauma warps our fundamental belief systems - beliefs about ourselves, others, and the world - and it is possible that our self-doubt is part of the PTSD.

Have you ever done something before that was hard or you felt was impossible at the time? Is it possible that your belief system might be undermining your attempts to make changes? Would you be willing to try to see if you are stronger than you think you are?

Lastly, we need to introduce the elephant in the room:

> **There are many of us reading this who don't believe we deserve to recover.**

In counseling hundreds of patients, we have come to see that this belief is not an outlier.

In the types of trauma chapter, we talked about Moral Injury. Remember that **Moral Injury is soul damage**. Because of the shame involved, we often can't talk about what happened, so **we can resort to punishing ourselves**.

Sometimes, this self-punishment comes in the form of choosing not to get the treatment we need. We sometimes tell ourselves that we don't deserve to have a life because of what we believe we did or didn't do. We may feel a form of survivor's guilt or tell ourselves that we don't deserve to get better because we are responsible for what happened.

So, we're going to ask you this instead:

Is it possible that you're wrong?

My friend, if you believe that getting treatment is a cop-out or the "easy way" to do things, you need to read on and learn about evidence-based treatment methods.

175

PTSD treatment is the very definition of taking responsibility; it requires us to stare into the belly of the beast, take full responsibility for our choices, and come face to face with our Truth.

The Truth will set you free - and maybe not in the way you expect.

We understand the existential desire to punish ourselves, but it's likely that you are not seeing your experience from an objective, third-person perspective.

If you believe you don't deserve to get better, that's okay—but we're challenging you to verify that by seeking the truth. Get treatment and then make an informed decision. If you're still hopped up on punishing yourself afterwards, at least you'll be certain why.

But here's the thing, friend: if you've come across one thing in this book that has surprised you so far, it's possible you're wrong about a lot of other stuff, too. Remind us of what you have to lose by getting treatment?

CHAPTER 6 REAL TALK ON SUICIDE

Trigger Warning: Many people with PTSD have thoughts about suicide, so as uncomfortable as this chapter might be, we have to discuss it.

- Among people who have had a diagnosis of PTSD in their lifetime, approximately 27% have also attempted suicide.
- Women with Post-Traumatic Stress Disorder (PTSD) are nearly seven times more likely than other women to die by suicide.
- The average time between PTSD diagnosis and suicide was less than two and a half years[133].

First responders who go to suicide calls have gruesome tales. They know that suicides seldom end the way a person hopes, especially since most of us are high or drunk when we make the attempt.

It is a violent, messed-up way to die, and everyone who is suicidal already knows that. We *know* this, yet we still think about it.

Suicidal thoughts are an unbelievably normal part of PTSD.

Normal doesn't mean that they are pleasant; it just means that we can expect this with PTSD - and we need to talk about it because it is the norm and not the exception.

If you are having suicidal thoughts right now, please contact the National Suicide Prevention Lifeline

1-800-273-8255
https://suicidepreventionlifeline.org/

The Lifeline provides 24/7, free and confidential support for people in distress.

Listen, We're not trying to read you. We've experienced this and heard this echoed a thousand times with clients.

We're going to talk about suicide in a way that acknowledges that many of us with PTSD have either tried to commit suicide or have seriously considered it, ourselves included. It's uncomfortable, but because nothing less than your life is at stake, we won't apologize for what we have to say. Buckle in.

Let's go back to that feelings continuum:

We remember that things on this feelings continuum attenuate from both ends in equal measure. When we avoid those crappy feelings on the left, we become *unable* to feel the good feelings we want on the right. We end up feeling right in the middle: numb.

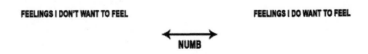

Numb is a frightening feeling. We know we should feel something, and we *actually* feel nothing. We may start to ask ourselves questions like, "what is wrong with me?" or "am I a sociopath?" Maybe we start to believe that we will never be "normal" again. We just feel nothing; no joy, no sadness—just numb.

Then we get an idea: I can end all of this by committing suicide. Suddenly we feel *something*—and this is a shock to us because we've felt nothing, absolutely nothing, for a long time. It feels *good*—not because the idea of schwacking ourselves isn't gruesome, but because we *feel something* again.

With suicide, we may not have the right answer, but we have something new. This may give us a little boost in our spirits, maybe some pep in our step. Our spouse may comment to us that we seem different or our colleagues may say, "it's good to see you smiling," and only we know why. All this external validation feels good, and we start thinking suicide may not be such a bad idea after all.

When therapists talk with a surviving loved one after a suicide, they often hear the same phrases over and over:

They seemed to be doing so much better lately.

I saw them smiling and participating in activities.

We thought the worst was over.

The suicide surprised them because they only saw what was present on the outside.

Sometimes we use thinking about suicide as a coping mechanism, or a strategy that we use in the face of stress to help us manage.

We may draft the suicide letter we will write, or fantasize

about who will be at our memorial, or imagine the ways our family and loved ones will be "better off" once we are gone.

Here's the thing, like other coping mechanisms, it *works*. Thinking about suicide can make us feel better and reinforce our belief that suicide is a good idea, even when we know it's not.

We may be telling ourselves, "I'm not going to actually do it, I just think about it." We fantasize about it more and more until we are thinking about suicide all the time. Inevitably, the stress we experience exceeds our capacity to manage it, and we begin to grasp for solutions - any solutions.

"It all happened so fast" is the number one phrase heard after a suicide attempt. We were likely under the influence of alcohol or drugs, and with PTSD, we are **literally** not in our right minds. And it goes down fast:

Before I knew it, I had the gun in my mouth.

Before I knew it, I was tying the noose.

Before I knew it, the bottle of pills was gone.

We need to be real: fantasy can turn into action at a frightening pace.

We may be telling ourselves that we'll never actually commit suicide, but it's hard to get off a moving train once we feel overwhelmed.

Suicidality doesn't always look like sticking a gun in our mouths. It can be reckless behavior, mad drinking, or drug use.

This is what we need you to know:

> **When we are using thoughts of suicide as a coping mechanism, we are closer to a tipping point than we think. It's time to get help.**

Suicide: The Forever Decision by Paul G. Quinnett is free to read online and an amazing resource if you are thinking about suicide in any way. Links are in the resource section at the back of this book.

You are not the only person who has thought of suicide or made an attempt in the face of PTSD. This is hard, but as Dr. Quinnett says, suicide is a forever decision.

We've already learned that our PTSD symptoms can fundamentally alter our psyche and our belief systems. Given this, it is highly likely that we are not seeing things for what they are, but we are seeing everything *through the lens of PTSD.*

In other words, it is possible that we are wrong.

Yup, we said it. You could be wrong, friend. Donkey Kong wrong.

We might have convinced ourselves that everyone will be better off if we kill ourselves, and maybe we are wrong, and our death will be a nightmare.

We may think we are beyond help, and maybe we are wrong because we don't know what we don't know.

You might have more grit and determination inside you than you think.

We know you're tired. PTSD is exhausting. But...

Maybe your healing will make you stronger; it might make your family stronger. Maybe—*maybe*—you're reading this for a reason. Maybe we don't need to do this anymore. Change is possible; maybe it's time.

---

[133] Suicide risk in people with post-traumatic stress disorder: A cohort study of 3.1 million people in Sweden. Fox, V., Dalman, C., Dal, H., Hollander, A.C., Kirkbride, J.B., Pitman, A. Journal of Affective Disorders Volume 279, 15 January 2021, Pages 609-616 https://www.sciencedirect.com/science/article/pii/S0165032720328536

CHAPTER 7 SOLUTIONS

When it comes to PTSD treatment, there are lots of opinions, and you know what they say about opinions; *"everyone has one, and most of them stink."* And to add insult to injury, most of these opinions have the word "just" to indicate how easy people think they are:

You just need to exercise more.

You just need to cut out gluten.

You just need to pray.

Before you write us a strongly worded email, we're not saying that getting off your butt, cutting carbs, and getting with God is a bad idea. In fact, we don't think anyone is being malicious when they give their opinion or say what worked for them. We trust Evidence-Based Treatments.

Here's the thing, we talked about these kinds of Toxic Positivity statements in an earlier chapter (See Types of Trauma-Other Issues). They come from a place of uncertainty. The person giving this advice doesn't know how to help you, but they want to feel like they are helpful.

If you want real help, it is going to come from a licensed therapist in the form of an Evidence-based treatment (EBTs).

EBTs are based on peer-reviewed scientific evidence. This means that researchers have conducted rigorous studies using scientific methods, documented their research in peer-reviewed publications, and then other researchers have conducted additional studies to see if the treatment is, in fact, successful. Unlike anecdotes, a ton of time and research goes into verifying that EBTs work. There is verifiable proof of this. EBTs work **most of the time for most people**, and they do so in about 12 sessions.

Three of the most commonly-employed Evidence-Based Treatments for PTSD are:

- **Prolonged Exposure Therapy (PE)**
- **Cognitive Processing Therapy (CPT)**
- **Eye-Movement Desensitization and Reprocessing (EMDR)**

We encourage you to ask for these EBTs by name and be insistent. There is no sense in working with a therapist who is not specifically trained in how to treat PTSD; it's a waste of time and leads to even more frustration.

Researchers know that there is a certain percentage of folks whose PTSD won't respond to these three EBTs. That doesn't mean that you're beyond hope, it just means we need to find another avenue of approach. There is a lot of money in PTSD research, and a lot of good clinical trials and solutions to try.

As of this writing, here are some of the treatments for treatment-resistant PTSD being used:

- The stellate ganglion block (sometimes called the "God Shot")
- Ketamine
- Marijuana
- Hallucinogens like MDMA
- Couples' therapy

Various treatments that help with PTSD and co-occurring disorders like depression, alcohol use, anger, anxiety, and TBIs.

This list is by no means exhaustive; researchers are learning more every day, and the ones I know care deeply about all of our troops and veterans. For more alternatives for those who are serving or have served in the military, talk to an expert on PTSD and keep up on the research through projects like STRONG STAR.

For now, we're going to assume that you have not tried any EBTs yet. Since most EBTs work for most people, we're going to explain each of the treatments to help you make an informed decision. Therapy is not easy, but it's not forever, either.

PROLONGED EXPOSURE THERAPY (PE)

PE Therapy typically takes 10-15 sessions with a therapist; each session is 90 minutes. PE therapy goes right for the jugular of criterion C of PTSD: avoidance.

Rather than avoid our trauma, we intentionally invite the most traumatic event into the session using a technique called "imaginal exposure." After learning breathing techniques to manage anxiety, we imagine and describe the traumatic event in detail with guidance from a therapist. After the imaginal exposure, we process the experience with our therapist. We audio record the session while describing the event so that we can listen to the recording between sessions; this helps us to further process our emotions and practice breathing techniques. Think of the imaginal exposure like this: it's like watching a horror movie.

When we first watch a horror movie, it scares the crap out of us because that's what horror movies do. What if we watch the horror movie back-to-back three times? It's still going to be scary, but, after the third time, we know what is coming and when, so it's not as bad as the first time.

What if we watch that horror movie ten times? Twenty times? A hundred times? Eventually, watching that movie doesn't affect us as much because we've seen it so many times and we know what's coming. This is called habituation; a decrease in response to a stimulus after repeated presentations.

In PE therapy, we'll be watching our horror movie literally hundreds of times—in session with our therapist and in between sessions by listening to our recordings.

The second part of PE therapy is called *in vivo exposure*, a fancy term for "in real life." With our therapist, we make a list of stimuli and situations connected to our trauma, such as specific places or people, and create a plan to intentionally expose ourselves to these stimuli in a way that is gradual and safe.

We realize that the thought of retelling our experience out loud can be anxiety-provoking. It's tough, especially at the start, but PE therapy is undeniably effective. It also can be adapted into treatment for Moral Injury, which we'll talk about later in this chapter.

PE therapy isn't for everyone, and that's okay because we're discussing three available EBTs, not just one. Here's the second:

COGNITIVE PROCESSING THERAPY (CPT)

CPT typically takes 12 sessions with a therapist; each session is 60 minutes. CPT can be done individually or in group sessions, and it uses a workbook for written assignments. *Cognitive* means that we pay attention to our thoughts and *think about what we are thinking about.*

CPT recognizes that trauma warps our fundamental belief systems—beliefs about ourselves, others, and the world—and that those warped beliefs affect our walking, talking, everyday lives.

In CPT, we learn about the relationship between thoughts and emotions and then learn to identify the automatic thoughts that maintain our PTSD symptoms.

We write an "impact statement" that details our understanding of why the traumatic event occurred and what impact it has had on our belief systems. Next, we'll use workbook exercises to identify and address unhelpful thinking patterns related to safety, trust, power and control, esteem, and intimacy. Our therapist will ask questions and work with us to recognize unhelpful thinking patterns, reframe our thoughts, reduce our symptoms, and come to a better understanding about ourselves and our relationships.

CPT forces us to get out of "auto-pilot" and start challenging our thought patterns.

Often these are thoughts we have held on to for a long time.

EYE-MOVEMENT DESENSITIZATION AND REPROCESSING (EMDR)

This description is from the good folks at the EMDR Institute, found online at www.emdr.com, and we encourage you to find a therapist who practices EMDR to give you a better description than the one provided.

EMDR is an eight-phase treatment that focuses attention on three distinct time periods: the past, present, and future. Sessions often last between 60-90 minutes.

The eight phases include:

History-taking: In this phase, the therapist obtains a detailed history of the client's past memories and current struggles. During this phase, the therapist will try and identify targets for the EMDR processing (these can be distressing memories or incidents).

Client preparation: This is where the client learns techniques for active healing trauma processing. The therapist will go over strategies, suggest relaxation techniques, and other coping strategies that can help their client deal with emotional distress and maintain improvements as the sessions progress.

Assessment: In this phase, the client is asked to picture an image closely related to the target memory and to elicit the negative response and beliefs associated with the memory. The client is also asked to identify a positive belief that they would like to believe instead.

Desensitization: The therapist asks their client to focus on a specific memory, belief, or emotional trigger while simultaneously engaging in bilateral stimulation (BLS). BLS consists of alternating right and left stimulation, whether it's tapping of the toes or tapping on the shoulders. It can also include audio or visual stimulation with the use of light. This stimulation may include eye movements, taps, or tones.

It is believed that BLS used in EMDR activates both hemispheres of the brain, which is believed to have a soothing effect, and dim the intensity of the memory while allowing the client space to process it without an overwhelming psychological response. This continues until that memory is no longer triggering for the client.

Installation: With the help of the therapist, this is where the client starts to replace negative thoughts with positive ones. Continuing to review the triggering memory with BLS, the client is asked to assess the emotional response and rate it against the positive belief (brought up during the assessment phase) they would prefer to associate it with.

Body scan: Here, the client is assessed for changes in body sensations when thinking of the negative incident and positive thought. Any remaining tension in the body is targeted by the therapist for additional processing.

Closure: Client's will be asked to write down any thoughts or emotions that arise during the coming week, and will be reminded of the self-soothing techniques they learned during the session in order to process any negative thoughts that may surface.

Reevaluation: This phase is to review and/or assess for other targets that cause distressing emotion within the chosen memory.

THE BOTTOM LINE

Don't stress out about which EBT to choose. Most cognitive-behavior therapies for PTSD work by exposing clients repeatedly to anxiety-provoking stimuli, either in their imagination (imaginal exposure) or in real life (in vivo exposure). When exposure to either type is sufficiently prolonged, clients' anxiety dissipates.

If we try one and it doesn't work, we have two more to fall back on. If we try all three and they don't work, we may be dealing with complex PTSD, treatment-resistant PTSD, or have co-occurring disorders to work through. Do not lose hope, this simply means we have a little more work to do with our treatment professional to come up with a more targeted course of action.

CHAPTER 8 PERSISTENCE

Numerous factors influence treatment outcomes, and no single treatment, or evidence-based treatment has demonstrated 100% effectiveness for every single person with PTSD. That doesn't mean recovery is hopeless. It's just going to take a little more work.

Let's go back to those earlier questions from chapter 5.

> 1. Do I believe change is possible?
> 2. Do I want to change?

The goal of this book is to help you heal, but you have to be willing, even when it is tough. We know you don't want to hear that, and believe us when we say, we empathize. That also means we know sugarcoating or trying to downplay the possibility that PTSD treatments might take a little longer than expected is not doing you any favors.

If *"knowing is half the battle,"* we want you to win the war.

And that means arming you with all the facts so you can get the help you need.

So, what could be delaying our recovery? The type and duration of trauma seems to play a part in the success of recovery.

It is also common for PTSD to be accompanied by comorbid psychiatric conditions, including depression, substance use disorders, and somatic symptoms making diagnosing the correct type of PTSD and any associating conditions key in unlocking the correct combination of treatments.

We realize that the idea of going through treatment for PTSD and still having to do more work is frustrating. Having more work to do doesn't mean we failed; it just means we have more work to do and that's okay.

Be easier on yourself; Rome wasn't built in a day.

C-PTSD

As we mentioned earlier, C-PTSD is not included in the DSM-5. For this reason, we want to make a note of it here, especially as it relates to what could be viewed as treatment-resistant PTSD (TR-PTSD).

PTSD and C-PTSD are similar in their root causes, with the C- distinction reflecting the repetitive nature of the trauma experienced over a long period of time.

People who have survived complex trauma, especially the trauma of sexual abuse, often display similar symptoms as those who live with Borderline Personality Disorder.

Common symptoms include severe depression, mood swings, anger, extreme feelings of loneliness and anxiety. Those who live with these symptoms can be seen as having difficulty regulating their emotions.

This often leads to a diagnosis, especially in women, of Borderline Personality Disorder.

C-PTSD is often misdiagnosed as Borderline Personality Disorder. The two share overlapping symptoms with one key difference, their attachment-style triggered reactions[134].

With Borderline Personality Disorder, the attachment style is one of needing someone to react to. They are hypervigilant about signs of rejection. Their fragmented sense of self is unstable and comes from a base of profound emotional emptiness with fears of being abandoned.

With C-PTSD, the attachment style is not based on fear of abandonment. It is a more relational detachment style. In other words, they would prefer to be left alone in many cases. Their hypervigilance is based on safety. It is easier to keep the peace in their lives if they do not have to risk getting close enough to someone who could hurt them.

While C-PTSD can be a severe and debilitating disorder, C-PTSD treatments do exist and are effective. Recovery from C-PTSD is a long process that often involves the standard treatments for PTSD (cognitive processing of the trauma), as well as additional psychotherapy to work with assistance for emotional regulation, skill building to overcome learned behaviors and habits that formed during the duration of the trauma, and Somatic psychotherapy to help retrain the nervous system to function and respond appropriately instead of defaulting to stress responses.

This is especially important if the trauma experienced began during childhood.

CO-OCCURRING DISORDERS

This is when we are diagnosed with two, or more, simultaneously occurring conditions. This is unbelievably common with PTSD. For example, we'll have PTSD and a substance or alcohol abuse problem at the same time, or PTSD and depression.

---

[134] Ford, J.D., Courtois, C.A. Complex PTSD and borderline personality disorder. Bord personal disord emot dysregul 8, 16 (2021). https://doi.org/10.1186/s40479-021-00155-9

CHAPTER 9 HOW TO FIND HELP

Now that we understand PTSD and the Evidence-Based Treatments that help, we need to find someone to help us create and execute a plan of action.

FINDING A THERAPIST

We understand that many of us do not relish the idea of going to therapy (the terms "therapy" and "counseling" are largely interchangeable). We might have the idea that we'll have to lie down on a couch and talk about our mommy issues, or maybe we think therapy is only for crazy people.

Obviously, we'd prefer to do it on our own rather than find a therapist. We get that, but there is tremendous value in **NOT** doing this alone, and instead working with a licensed mental health professional. It is valuable to get feedback from someone who can provide an objective, third-person perspective, that is 100% on our side, and sincerely wants what is best for us.

Moreover, our therapist is not our friend. This is a good thing to understand because a therapist can tell us what we *need* to hear instead of what we *want* to hear.

Our therapist will not always agree with us and will often challenge our understanding, point out negative self-talk, and ask us tough questions.

The word "therapist" is a generic term for someone who conducts therapy with clients. Many mental health professionals fall into this category. If possible, we recommend finding a licensed therapist with specialized training in treating PTSD; a specialist, and not a generalist.

When someone has cancer, they don't go to their family doctor for treatment; they go to an oncologist: someone who specializes in cancer. When our life is on the line, we want the best possible treatment. The same is true for mental health: therapists tend to specialize in specific treatment methods or specific client populations.

For example, Virginia focuses on combat-related PTSD and Moral Injury. While she can do other things, it's not what she's best at. She has amazing colleagues who specialize in eating disorders, adolescent-issues, depression, anxiety, and all manner of mental health issues, and if you come into her office with an experience that is better addressed with one of her colleagues, she will refer you to them.

Finding a therapist who specializes in PTSD and has training in an evidence-based treatment for PTSD is smart, but it isn't always easy. To find a PTSD specialist, we can get help from our health insurer's website, or use our company's employee assistance program (EAP). We can also find therapists on the internet by searching by the name of the evidence-based treatment and with our zip code (for example, "EMDR therapist Tampa 33607").

Once we find a therapist, we can call and request a phone consultation with them. Keep in mind that we may call and leave messages with several providers, but may only hear back from a few. (Therapists can be crappy this way.)

During the phone consult:

1. Briefly explain why we are seeking therapy.

2. Ask what experience they have treating clients like us.

3. Ask if they are trained in Evidence-Based Treatments for PTSD/Moral Injury.

This may sound like,

"I'm trying to cope with the trauma and fallout of my abusive marriage. What kind of treatment do you use for PTSD?"

If the therapist does not have training in an evidence-based treatment for PTSD, ask them if they can recommend someone who does.

Next, we'll make our first appointment. It's okay to feel nervous; in this first session, we are getting to know the therapist and trying to determine if it is a relationship that will last.

It also might not be. Not all therapists are compatible with all clients, and that's okay. The relationship between a client and their therapist is important. We need to feel a sense of trust with our therapist because we have to choose to be authentic in order to improve.

Some therapists are unprofessional or simply not good at their jobs. We're not trying to be ugly; it is what it is. If you don't click with your therapist, it's not necessarily you. Keep looking - there is excellent advice online about how to choose the best therapist.

Having a therapist we can trust is an important cornerstone for our social support network and is vital to our recovery.

TALK TO YOUR THERAPIST ABOUT CONFIDENTIALITY

The Health Insurance Portability and Accountability Act (HIPAA) contains a privacy rule that creates national standards to protect individuals' medical records and personal health information, including information about psychotherapy and mental health. The HIPAA Privacy Rule is a limited level of protection only.

Confidentiality is one reason therapy works. Therapists understand that for people to feel comfortable talking about private and revealing information, they need a safe place to talk about anything, without fear of that information leaving the room, and they take patient confidentiality seriously. However, the limits of confidentiality in counseling stop whenever a client expresses the intent to harm themselves or others. In those situations, the therapist is legally obligated to break confidentiality.

According to the privacy and confidentiality section of the APA's ethical code of conduct for therapists[135], there are four general situations which are exempt from confidentiality:

- The client is an imminent and violent threat towards themselves or others.
- There is a billing situation which requires a condoned disclosure.
- Sharing information is necessary to facilitate client care across multiple providers.
- Sharing information is necessary to treat the client.

At your first visit, the therapist should give you information that explains their privacy policies and how your personal information will be handled.

This information will explain that, in some cases, there are exceptions to the privacy rule:

- The therapist may disclose private information without consent in order to protect the patient or the public from serious harm — if, for example, a client discusses plans to attempt suicide or harm another person.
- The therapist is required to report ongoing domestic violence, abuse or neglect of children, the elderly, or people with disabilities.
- The therapist may release information if they receive a court order.

A good therapist should be happy to go over any confidentiality concerns with you before starting therapy. Ask any questions at that time, to put your mind at ease. Some questions we suggest asking are:

- Who will have access to your clinical notes?
- What do you report to your health insurance?
- What is the level of detail you will document in medical records?

We encourage asking for a copy of your medical records. You should read them too.

Remember, your therapist should be transparent. If they are not, it's time to find a new therapist.

A WORD ON SUPPORT GROUPS AND GROUP THERAPY

Support groups are often led by paraprofessionals rather than licensed therapists.

We're HUGE proponents of group therapy.

Before sharing your Truth, we encourage you to (1) ensure that your group is run by an experienced group leader, preferably a <u>Certified Group Psychotherapist</u>, and (2) to discuss confidentiality with your therapist and with your therapy group.

THE BOTTOM LINE

We cannot guarantee confidentiality in groups because other group members are not mental health professionals required to follow the rules of ethics in order to keep a state license. Unfortunately, this makes sharing our Truth in groups a risk we must seriously consider.

HOW TO GET MENTAL HEALTH HELP WITHOUT INSURANCE

- A distressingly large number of people with mental health issues have little to no insurance. [136]
- 11.1% of Americans with a mental illness are uninsured.
- 8.1% of children have private insurance that does not cover mental health services.
- In 2019, 24.7% of adults with a mental illness reported an unmet need for treatment.
- Over half of adults with a mental illness do not receive treatment, totaling over 27 million untreated adults in the U.S.

The sad truth is, many Americans struggle to pay for expensive mental health treatment without insurance, often without cash on hand.

There is help out there.

Please use the following listing to get you started.

The Substance Abuse and Mental Health Assistance (SAMHSA) National Helpline
1-800-662-HELP (4357).
*This resource is **free, confidential, and staffed by professional volunteers** who can talk you through a crisis and/or connect you with nearby resources that can help.*
https://www.samhsa.gov/find-help/national-helpline

The National Alliance on Mental Illness
1-800-950-6264.
You can also text "NAMI" to 741741 on a smartphone.
*NAMI operates a **toll-free helpline for people who need to get mental health help with no insurance.***
You can reach NAMI online at https://nami.org/Home

National Suicide Prevention Lifeline
1-800-273- TALK (8255).
*On July 16, 2020, the FCC adopted rules to establish **988** as the new, nationwide, 3-digit phone number Americans can use to connect with suicide prevention and mental health crisis counselors. By **July 16, 2022,** phone service providers will be required to direct all **988** calls to the existing National Suicide Prevention Lifeline.* Until then, please continue to use 1-800-273-8255.

Employee Assistance Program.
Hear us out—We think this is one of the most underutilized work benefits and it is widely available to almost anyone employed, even on a part-time basis.

EAPs are part of many benefits packages, and a call to your Human Resources folks will give you more information. An EAP is a work-based intervention program designed to identify and assist employees in resolving personal problems that may be adversely affecting their performance at work. EAPs offer free short-term counseling to employees and family members, and the EAP will usually set you up with a counselor, making it user friendly.

Many EAPs give clients five-to-ten therapy sessions with no cost or co-pay. If you have a high deductible before your insurance kicks in, EAP is a good option.

Call 211.

This is the nationwide, non-emergency referral service for state and community services. Through 211, people can find out about resources that may help with healthcare costs; however, this is not a hotline. Some healthcare concerns 211 resource specialists can help locate resources for include:

- Access to affordable healthcare, including locating clinics that are free, low-cost, or work on a sliding scale
- Lower cost mental health and counseling options
- Programs to provide financial assistance to pay medical bills
- Transportation services to help individuals get medical treatment
- Information on local agencies that can assist in prescription costs or pharmaceutical programs for medication assistance
- Services for substance abuse, including counseling and treatment programs

If you attend a college or university, check with the health center to find out what counseling services they offer. If you don't attend, but have universities and colleges in your area, call to see if they have a psychology department. They might provide a reduced rate or a sliding-scale therapy with clinician-supervised students training to become psychologists or therapists.

Call around and speak to **local mental health professionals**. See if they will work on a sliding- scale, or ask for their recommendations. Folks who work in mental health all tend to hang out together and are usually very connected to our local community resources.

Lastly, try contacting a **social worker in a government agency or hospital** and ask them. In our experience, we have found that social workers have a unique superpower: knowing things. They are super humanly resourceful.

---

[135] APA's Ethical Principles of Psychologists and Code of Conduct. https://www.apa.org/ethics/code/

[136] The State Of Mental Health In America https://www.mhanational.org/issues/state-mental-health-america

CHAPTER 10 SOCIAL SUPPORT

THE KEY TO LASTING CHANGE

"Social Support." This is what mental health professionals call "friends" and researchers have shown over and again the importance of social support in treating PTSD. Our therapist is part of our support team, and we have to build on this foundation. Making friends is difficult, especially if we have PTSD. So, let's talk about it...

Back in the day, making friends was easy. As a kid, we made friends in school or in our neighborhood, and in the military, we have/had our unit. Making friends gets harder as we get older. We realize that for guys, it's weird to approach another dude and say, "want to hang out?"

Women are different in this regard, but we also tend to isolate ourselves in the face of PTSD, saying things like, "I don't want to bother them with this. they have their own crap they're going through. My friends are just all so busy. I don't want them to think I'm a drama bomb."

Real talk, if you would drop everything for a friend that is going through what you are going through, then give them the same respect to come and help you.

Even when we know that making friends and building networks helps us recover from PTSD, it is an anxiety-inducing idea.

Some people are natural extroverts (and yay for you), but normal people worry about making new friends, especially if our PTSD has poisoned our other relationships. It's normal to worry.

"What if new people learn about my PTSD and freak out? What if I have a melt-down, or if I hurt someone by accident? Maybe I'm better off protecting the world by keeping to myself because people have their own problems and they don't need mine."

We hear you, friend, and want to put this into perspective. Trying to make friends is a big risk. We can be rejected, others can judge us and be crappy, and we might be terrible at making new friends—but we also know that social support is a major determining factor in our recovery from PTSD. In other words, to get better, this is a risk we *need* to take.

Because this is important, we want to take you back to the Big Two questions. (Q1) Do we believe it's possible? Do we believe it's possible that we could get out of our comfort zone, break out of that Criterion C of avoidance, and connect with another person, either in-person or virtually? Is it possible that there is another person in this world who is not crappy? Is it possible that we can use this powerful—and proven—tool of social support to fight our PTSD symptoms? Is it possible that we deserve to be loved and cared for by others? (This last one is hard with all that Criterion D negative self-talk rattling around in our brains. We're just asking if it's *possible*.)

Trust is hard, especially if, in our past, we've tried to connect with someone for support and they fucked us over.

Moving on to (Q2) "Do we want to change?"

But rephrasing it differently. The second question can't be, "Do we want to make friends?" Because we already know the answer: NO. With PTSD, we *want* to avoid other people. This is good old criterion C: avoidance. It's like asking, "do we want to go to therapy?" Big NO. So, we need to look at the bigger picture of Q2. Do we want to do the work it will take to recover from PTSD? Do we want to lessen our symptoms? Do we want the people we love *to know* that we love them? Do we want to build, and possibly rebuild, relationships?

It's okay to be on the struggle bus about this. Going to therapy and making connections is difficult when we have PTSD, but we have to do it if we are serious about getting our lives back. Let's talk about how to do this.

DIFFERENT KINDS OF FRIENDS

When we think about friends, we tend to put them in two categories: (1) lifelong, know everything about me, ride or die friends, and (2) acquaintances. Maybe we work with them, and that's about it.

For the purpose of making new friends, we want to introduce a new relationship into our lexicon:

The In-Between Friend:
Not a life-long ride or die friend, and not that weird guy at the office, but someone in-between.

As adults, the way we build social support is by making in-between friends.

In-between friends start out just like us; they are other people who are also trying to find social support. Not every in-between friend will turn into a lifelong ride or die friend; in fact, most won't - but some of them will. It's the law of averages: the more in-between friends we make, the better the chances of that friendship developing into a ride or die friendship.

We recommend that we make this our course of action for building social support. There is little pressure when making in-between friends because the way we find them is to *intentionally go* to places where other people are trying to make in-between friends. We go intending to connect with other like-minded people, and, over time, there is a likelihood that we will *regularly connect* with them.

First things first: what are places or events where people intentionally come together because they want connection?

These are smaller groups (maybe 5-10 people) in which it is likely we will be individually noticed and talk to someone else because it would be hard not to. Everyone attends the group because we all have the intention of connecting with others who have shared values and interests.

These are places where *individuals* come together, not couples or groups of friends.

Sure, we will be the new person the first time we visit the group, but everyone else will have had that same experience at one time. It is largely their role to engage you because they remember how awkward it was for them the first time.

Also, we are looking for groups where there is a **planned activity**.

207

This eliminates anxiety-provoking small talk and the desire to drink or use to feel more comfortable. We don't have to talk about ourselves because we can talk about the activity, and focusing on that activity keeps us from thinking about our PTSD. There is little pressure.

Here is a non-exhaustive list of ideas for finding small groups:

MEETUP

Meetup is a service used to organize online groups that host in-person events for people with similar interests and has over 35 million members. Their motto is, "we are what we do," and the groups are activity-based. We can look up groups in our area from the comfort and anonymity of the internet at www.meetup.com.

Book clubs, hiking groups, music nerds, museum visiting groups, and pretty much anything you can think of. Their purpose is to meet people in person and spend time together sharing an activity. Fun fact: I found a photography meetup group in Paris a few years back. They even have an app for smart phones.

CIVIC GROUPS

These are organizations that promote civic or social interests and are often supported by a group of members. Examples are Rotary International, Shriners, Toastmasters, and Veterans groups like the American Legion or the VFW. Civic groups often support service projects and have guest speakers and networking events.

PROFESSIONAL ORGANIZATIONS

These groups often have networking events rather than specific activities. If shoptalk comes easier to us than feelings-talk, this is a good place to start. Google a specific profession or interest with the phrase "professional organization." Examples are the Veterans Business Network, the National Association for Women Business Owners, the Gay and Lesbian Medical Association, and the National Society of Black Engineers. Local chapters abound.

PLACES OF WORSHIP

Churches, synagogues, ashrams, mosques, and even meet up groups for atheists and agnostics are all places where people come together with a shared belief system. Many places of worship have smaller groups of 5-10 people where we can meet others for a shared activity. Examples are religious study groups, reading groups, home cell groups, choirs and creative arts groups, and community volunteer groups.

Many places of worship have websites and calendars advertising their group events. If not, we recommend looking up the phone number and asking to speak with someone.

Try this script: "Hi, I'm looking to learn more about your organization and was wondering if you have a small group or event during the week that I could check out to meet some new people."

VOLUNTEERING

Not good with people at all? Us, too. Virginia walks dogs at the local animal shelter and meets other folks who prefer canines to humans.

Volunteering is a great way to meet people who care about the same things we do. We can volunteer to build houses for Vets or organize for social justice.

SUPPORT GROUPS

Support groups bring together people who are going through similar experiences; they are often led by paraprofessionals rather than licensed therapists, and the focus is on listening and working together as a group to heal and grow.

Visitors are welcome to share as little or as much as they like.

Support groups can be powerful because it reminds us that we are not alone and that others have also persevered through challenges. Support groups can help us feel less isolated, especially when we can relate to others in a similar situation.

NAMI.org lists support groups for mental health issues and SAMHSA.gov lists many resources for alcohol and substance use, as well as mental health and other important topics.

Survivors of Loved Ones' Suicides (SOLOS) is an especially powerful peer-led support group.

AA, NA, AL ANON, ETC.

12-step programs are powerful in terms of providing social support and accountability, and there are anonymous groups for many addictions. In addition to the three most widely known programs, Codependents Anonymous (CoDA) is a powerful change agent, as are groups for Gambling and Survivors of Incest. Not everyone is a fan of the program, and we get it—there are plenty of lousy groups and crappy sponsors. There are also dynamic, inspiring groups, and amazing sponsors. We can group hop until we find a group that suits us.

GROUP THERAPY

Therapy groups, unlike support groups, are led by licensed mental health professionals, and they can be effective methods of support. There are marked differences between group therapy and support groups.

Therapy groups tend to be small, with around eight group members and one or two group leaders. The leaders screen group members prior to members joining the group, and leaders are licensed mental health providers with group training. Group therapy is not free; it is sometimes covered by health insurance or members pay out of pocket. Groups can be online or in person. Group is hard work, and it's worth it.

INDIVIDUAL THERAPY

You knew this was coming. In terms of social support, our therapist should be our greatest champion.

They should provide us with an objective, third-person perspective and be 100% on our side. Our therapist is a sounding board, a safe person with whom we can brainstorm, and a resource.

ONLINE GROUPS

There is an impressive amount of social support available online in chat forums and social media groups. To find one, try using a search term like "online support group PTSD."

Once we find a group we might like, we have to commit to go. The next step is to attend regularly.

Our goal is to make in-between friends with a long-term goal of building a tribe of supporters. Tribes come with accountability. When we miss a book club meeting, our in-between friend will call to see if we're sick. When we miss a program meeting, our sponsor will call to see if we've relapsed.

We know that with PTSD we just want to be left alone, but others checking up on us is a good thing. It is the opposite of avoidance because we are intentionally inviting others into our world, even if it's only once a week.

THE BOTTOM LINE

Building a social support network is a leap of faith. It is also evidence-based in terms of helping us recover. When we believe change is possible and we want to change, we choose to act. So, (1) pick an activity, and (2) show up and just breathe. Everyone in the group has been the new person before; they get it.

CHAPTER 11 TALKING ABOUT OUR PTSD

Not everyone has earned the right to know our story, but there are probably some people in our lives who have. In this chapter, we're going to map out exactly how to talk to the people in our lives who matter. We will learn what to say and how to say it.

WE CONTROL THE NARRATIVE OR THE NARRATIVE CONTROLS US

SCIENCE

Let's start by showing you how powerful and transformative our narrative can be.

In 1964, Harvard professor Robert Rosenthal, conducted an experiment at an elementary school near San Francisco. He gave all the students a standardized IQ test, but put a new cover sheet on it, calling it the "Harvard Test of Inflected Acquisition." Just to be clear, *this was a lie*. It was a standard IQ test, but Rosenthal gave everyone the impression it was something new and fancy.

Rosenthal told the teachers that this fancy-dancy Harvard test had the ability to predict which kids were about to experience a dramatic growth in their IQ—special kids that were about to get dramatically smarter. Sounds impressive, right? Exactly. *Again: not true.*

After the kids took the test, Rosenthal chose kids completely at random and told their teachers that the test results predicted which kids were on the verge of an intense intellectual bloom. He told the teachers, but not the students. Rosenthal's team followed the children over the next two years, and at the end of the study, all students were tested again with the same IQ-test used at the beginning of the study. Something miraculous happened: the children Rosenthal labeled as "intellectual bloomers" did show statistically significant gains on the test.

Just one problem: these kids were picked at random. How did they experience such a shift in IQ? Rosenthal observed the students in the classroom and discovered that the teacher's expectations significantly affected the students. The teachers' moment-to-moment interactions with the children they expected to bloom differed from the students they considered "normal." Teachers gave the students they expected to succeed _more_ - more individual attention, more time to answer questions, and more affirmation and approval. "It's not magic, it's not mental telepathy," Rosenthal said. "It's very likely these thousands of different ways of treating people, in small ways, every day."

It was not the children's aptitude that gave them a statistically significant improvement in IQ. It was **their narrative**—the story their teachers **believed** about them.

LITERATURE

Let's think about stories that inspire us. Whether fiction or non-fiction, studies of literature tell us that inspirational stories have a similar pattern.

We can go all intel and graph it.

We'll call our x axis "time" and our y axis "level of happiness/success."

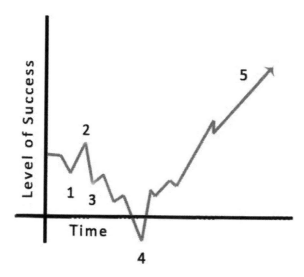

Follow the numbers on the graph and let us show you the basic structure of an inspirational story:

1. So, there I was, doing my own thing, and I failed.

2. I did what I could to get better, and it looked like it was working.

3. But I failed again. I tried and tried, and things get kept getting worse.

4. Finally, I hit "rock bottom" and everything went to hell. But at rock bottom, something miraculous happened: I had an epiphany! I learned something I didn't know before, met someone I hadn't met before, did something I'd never done before, and I learned and improved!

5. Because life is life, there were ups and downs, but, in general, my life kept going up and I lived happily ever after.

Generally, this is the pattern of stories of people that inspire us. Novelists know this, every Chicken Soup for the Soul book thrives on this, and we feel inspired when we learn about people whose lives fit into this pattern, too. Rocky Balboa, Oprah, Elon Musk - everyone loves an underdog, everyone loves to see a comeback.

Narratives inspire us and capture our imagination. In controlling our own narrative, we can tap into this power and use it to help gather support from our peers and loved ones as we recover from PTSD.

PSYCHOLOGY

Let's look at an entire school of therapy that focuses on narrative, called Logotherapy. It was developed by Viktor Frankl, a neurologist, psychiatrist, and Auschwitz survivor. Frankl knew that personal experiences are transformed into personal stories that are given meaning and help shape a person's identity.

Frankl understood that there are a lot of things in our lives that we don't get to choose. We don't choose our family or where we grow up; children have precious little autonomy. As adults, we don't always get a choice, either; Frankl certainly did not choose to be imprisoned in a concentration camp.

But Frankl knew that man is "capable of resisting and braving even the worst conditions," and, in doing such, we can detach from situations and from ourselves. Narrative Therapy, credited to Michael White and David Epston, also seeks to externalize situations from ourselves. The idea is that we can choose an attitude about ourselves and our trauma because we survived it.

When we survive it, we get to define it.

We say again: when we survive it, we get to define it. We get to define our trauma, its meaning, and how it shapes us. Nobody else has the right to define our experience because this is not a team sport.

When we tell our story, it is an action toward change. Through this third-person point of view, we can be more objective. We can have compassion for ourselves while boldly asking for that same compassion and support from others.

OPENING UP ABOUT OUR PTSD TO RECOVER OUR RELATIONSHIPS

This part is uncomfortable, and it should be. Our loved ones matter, and our PTSD has probably messed up some of our most important relationships. We are going to take ownership of our narrative and learn how to openly discuss our issues in a way that creates opportunities to recover our relationships.

Virginia has taught this subject hundreds of times over the last few years and created an "elevator speech." It's based on good science and she's seen it work time and again. We may think that our relationships are too far gone and that we are the one person who cannot make this chapter work, but we have nothing to lose and everything to gain by connecting or reconnecting with people who love us. We'll create a script, we'll choose to be uncomfortable and vulnerable, and we'll choose to roll the dice. This chapter won't tickle, but it will probably be effective.

"But, Virginia," you plead, *"you don't know what I've done to my relationships!"* And you're right. However, Virginia has seen this work enough times that she had to include it here. Just walk with us for a bit.

LET'S BEGIN

Awful things happen in our personal relationships when we have PTSD. Persistent negative beliefs about ourselves, other people, and the world are like a shotgun blast to our personal relationships.

This is true even with the people who we care about, and care about us, the most: a battle buddy, parent, spouse, child, or lifelong friend. We may not even realize we have PTSD when our relationships turn south.

Let's talk about the Big Ugly: we may not know we have PTSD, but we suspect something is off. We may feel like we're in a funk or not feeling like ourselves.

We know that something about us is different, and not in a good or cute way.

Our loved ones know something is off, too.

They may not know exactly what is wrong, but they know something is off.

And *we know they know* something is off.

And they know we know they know something is off.

Our PTSD becomes the metaphorical elephant in the room.

This means that there is something in the room that is obvious—everyone knows it's there, yet no one talks about it because it is too uncomfortable to do so.

Our PTSD is as obvious, distressing, and as awkward as a massive elephant in a small room. We know our loved ones are worried about us, and *they know we know*. Our loved ones may not want to upset us or make us feel suicidal by talking about our symptoms. They might not know what PTSD is, or maybe they are genuinely frightened about what might happen if they upset the balance by breaking the silence. We may not bring it up because *we know* our PTSD is stressing them out. W*e know* they are scared, and *we know* they don't know what to say. If we knew what to do, we would already have done it.

Rather than talk about our PTSD with the people we love the most, we choose to avoid them, and we're back to criterion C (avoidance) rearing its ugly head.

It's easy for us to fall into avoidance. It often starts with the best of intentions; we may try to spare our loved ones from our symptoms, or we may be frightened for their safety.

We jump into a shame spiral and isolate ourselves from the people who love us, and can support us the most. Maybe when we interact with others, we get angry or frustrated or lose it. And we might start drawing conclusions that aren't true, like that they are better off without us.

Here's the stubborn thing about love:
it doesn't give up easily.

Sometimes, our loved ones reach false conclusions, too. Without information, the brain fills in the gaps to explain why things are different.

Maybe we're not cool with meeting up in public because crowds freak us out. Our friend, on the other hand, thinks we're mad at them about something.

We don't go to the school play because we don't want to have a panic attack in public, and our child thinks it's because they didn't get a big enough part.

We don't read a bedtime story to our child because we don't want to cry in front of them. Meanwhile, our child thinks, "Mommy doesn't read to me anymore because I'm a bad kid."

We know this hurts to hear, and we're saying this to you with love:

> *In the absence of an explanation from us, our loves ones will reach conclusions all on their own. It will probably be dead wrong, and it will probably become another, bigger, uglier, smellier, more awkward elephant in the room that we all choose not to discuss.*

You may be reading this *after* the divorce was already finalized, or *after* we told someone we never wanted to speak with them again, or *after* the kids left for college. We get that our PTSD may have already sledge-hammered our relationships, but we want to talk about how to invite those relationships back.

THE ELEVATOR SPEECH

We get the term "elevator speech" from the business world. It's brief, about 30 seconds (the time it takes to ride from the bottom to the top of a building in an elevator).

Its intent is to clearly and succinctly state our purpose.

> Our elevator speech has 7 distinct parts:
>
> 1. Ask permission to speak without interruptions and wait for response
> 2. Introduce our elephant: own our emotions/lack of emotion, and let them know we're okay
> 3. Own our past - own our narrative, speak plainly
> 4. Describe our turning point - epiphany
> 5. Ask for buy-in and support; manage expectations
> 6. Love them
> 7. Silence

1. Ask permission. Before rolling out our elevator speech, it's important that we let our loved one know that we want to talk to them about something important, and we will need about 30 seconds of uninterrupted time to do it.

No questions, no interjections; just 30 seconds of them listening to us with an open mind.

It's important to recognize that not everyone we love will be on board for this, and that's okay.

Relationships take two people, and it is incredibly important that we choose to honor others' boundaries—because honoring someone else's boundaries is a way we show love and respect for them as a person.

We ask for permission right off the bat. It may sound like this:

"I'm thankful that we have this time alone together because there is something important I'd like to talk to you about. If it's okay, I'd like to say it all at once and I promise it will only take about 30 seconds. Would it be okay if I got this all out at once - with no questions?"

After asking permission, wait for a verbal yes. Only after that, proceed.

Let's say our loved one is an interrupter. That's okay. If they interrupt, just ask again, "Would it be okay with you if I got this all out? I promise I will answer any questions you have in about 30 seconds."

What if they say no?

This happens, and it's okay. Let them know that if they change their mind, we are available. Reaffirm that we care about them and respect their boundaries.

It may sound something like this:

"I completely understand, and I respect your boundaries. If you change your mind, please know that I would value talking with you."

Then, leave it alone. They will talk to you when they are ready.

2. Introduce our elephant. We believe that whenever there is an elephant in the room, we are smart to introduce it. We will probably have a lot of uncomfortable feelings when we choose to talk to our loved one—nervous, emotional, or frustrated.

We may feel completely numb and find it hard to connect. All of that is okay. We'll name our feelings and let our loved one know that we are all right. It may sound like this:

222

"I have to be honest with you. I feel really nervous talking to you right now. If I sound shaky, it's because I am, but I'll be okay."

Or,

"I realize I might sound like I'm not feeling anything right now. It's hard for me to connect, but I promise you that I want to."

3. Own our past. This is an opportunity for us to own our behavior and not make any excuses.

Let's remember that this is an elevator speech, so keep it concise. We cannot stress this enough: *keep it simple.* This is not making amends, this is not talking to our therapist, so keep it short and stay on point. There will be time to go in depth, and the time is not during our elevator speech.

Remember: if we are taking more than 60 seconds, we are doing it wrong.

This may sound like,

"I know that things have been off. I've been drinking too much and spending a lot of time alone."

Or,

"I've had a terrible couple of years. I've struggled with feeling down. I recognize that this has affected you, too."

Nothing we are saying is a revelation; we are simply naming another elephant in the room. We are telling our loved one that we've been struggling, and that we recognize they see it, too.

We don't have to go into it because they already know.

We must stress that this is _not_ the time to bring up anything new. Don't say,

223

"I've really had a hard time these past few years... which is why I'm having an affair."

Stupid hurts. Don't do that. When we've got a bomb to drop, do it with a licensed marriage and family therapist present.

4. The epiphany. An epiphany is the "a-ha!" moment.

We learned something we didn't know before, we saw something we didn't notice before, or we realized something we hadn't fully grasped before—and because of this, everything has shifted.

To use corporate jargon, we had a "paradigm shift" and our fundamental belief system has changed—or, for the first time, we want our fundamental belief system to change. Our Big Two has shifted: we either believe change is possible, or we want to change, and we are ready to take that next step.

It may sound like we're being flippant here, but this is no small deal. Epiphanies come in packages large and small, but their impact is profound. What was it that made us want to change? This can sound like,

"I realized after my last suicide attempt that I want to live,"

or,

"I decided that I want to be the best Mom I can be."

5. Ask for buy-in, manage expectations. This is when the conversation shifts to the here and now.

We need support from our loved one, and this is the time for us to ask for it. It is also the time for us to manage expectations: this journey will not be easy, but we are dedicated to trying. It may sound something like this,

"I'm here and I want to change, but I also know that this won't be easy and I'll probably screw up a lot. But I believe that with your continued support, I can do this."

Or maybe,

"Mommy has decided to get the help she needs to get better. It might take a while to see the changes in me, but I promise that I will keep trying, even if I mess up at first."

Coming back from PTSD is not an overnight process, and we need to let our loved ones know that we are all-in.

6. Love them. Not everyone is comfortable with those three little words, but this is our chance to break ranks. Yes, we have to say those words. Keep it simple:

"The most important thing I want you to know is that I love you and I'm open to answering any questions you have."

7. Silence. This is the hardest part of the elevator speech because every part of us wants to jump to the rescue or break the awkward silence. We implore you, friend: *Be Silent*.

Don't go in for the hug. Don't try to comfort or soothe. At this moment, we must choose to be silent.

This is our loved ones' time to speak, and we absolutely must respect that.

When we choose to be silent, it gives them an opportunity to feel whatever it is they feel without interjection and without judgment. Our silence honors their experience and it invites them to share their thoughts, feelings, and emotions with us.

This is our time to be in reception mode, and, yes, it feels vulnerable and frightening.

This is how we reconnect; it is an invitation for them to be with us in a radically authentic way.

Radical authenticity is scary because it means that we are evicting all the elephants and choosing to be honest, even if it's messy. In our elevator speech, we choose to be messy and honest, and, in our silence, we invite our loved one to be radically authentic with us. Again, it will be hard to stay silent, but it is vital.

Our loved one may not be ready to talk with us at that moment, and that's okay. They may be angry, or emotional, or completely unfazed—and it's all okay. We have opened a door that is not easily shut. From here, we can let them know that if they change their mind, we are available, and we reaffirm that we care about them and respect their boundaries. "I completely understand, and I respect your boundaries. If you change your mind, please know that I would value talking with you." They will talk to you when they are ready. That is when the real connection or reconnection is possible.

SOME NOTES

Every elevator speech is as different as our experiences, but it is important that we **follow the outline**. Virginia developed the elevator speech on the backs of work by Robert Rosenthal and Viktor Frankl, two greats in psychology, and this strategy has helped literally hundreds of clients reconnect with their loved ones and forge a path to recovery.

Use notes to help. Talking to our loved ones about our PTSD is a nerve-wracking experience. We encourage the use of written notes if that helps steady you.

226

Just be sure to let your loved one know you are going to use some notes to feel steady.

"But..." **I hear you saying,** *"this all sounds pretty manipulative."*

You may be right. Here's the deal, friend: there is no need to reinvent the wheel when we have good science and research available to us.

Our personal feelings are that the only way this is manipulative is if our words are inauthentic.

- **Place and space.**
  It's important that we choose an appropriate time and place to speak to our loved one if we have a choice. If we're incarcerated or in the hospital, our options are limited, but if we have more freedom, it's smart to use it. We recommend a quiet place without interruptions.
- **This is an individual conversation.**
  Maybe you have six children, including two sets of twins. Good on you, but this is not a time to load the Brady Bunch up on the couch for a family discussion. This is a one-on-one conversation. The reason is simple: our PTSD affects no two people the same, and it is important that we honor each individual experience. This is especially true for children; one child may be sensitive, and another may not care as much—and it's all okay.
- **You will probably cry.**
  Not a sweet, white handkerchief cry, but a big ugly cry. Be smart: have tissue on hand so you don't snot yourself. And maybe consider laying off the mascara so you don't look like the joker when those tears roll. If you don't cry, there is nothing wrong. Feeling numb is normal with PTSD and it's okay.

- **Keep it age appropriate**.

  We need to use language our loved one can understand. Our elevator speech with a parent will differ from our elevator speech with a child.

- **Practice.**

  We encourage role playing our elevator speech before going live. Trying it with a therapist or a trusted friend is great, and it will encourage us.

  If we don't have a social support network yet, saying our elevator speech out loud in front of a mirror will help ease anxiety and nerves.

- **Write it out.**

  Some of us have such overwhelming anxiety that the idea of talking to another person is just not in the cards for us right now. That's okay. Write your elevator speech in a letter and hand it to a loved one. It doesn't matter how we connect; it matters that we choose to connect.

Inside Tip

Need a pep talk on the power of vulnerability? Listen to Brené Brown's brilliant TED talk. She explains her research and how to use our vulnerability to truly connect with others.

Worth 15 minutes of your life.

SOME EXAMPLES

Here are some examples of elevator speeches to help us feel confident in formulating our own. Don't worry about screwing up. What matters is that we show up and choose to be present. Yes, we will feel vulnerable. Yes, we will feel awkward. Yes, we will feel afraid—but we choose to do it, anyway. Even if it goes to hell, we are choosing to be brave, and that is awesome.

EXAMPLE 1

Ask Permission

"Honey, I'm glad we have time alone tonight because there is something important that I would like to talk about. I promise it's not bad, but it is something that I need to get out all at once if that's okay. Would it be all right with you if I took 30 seconds to get this all out at once with no questions or interruptions?"

(STOP - wait for an answer.)

Introduce Our Elephant

"I took time to write some things down on this paper because I don't want to forget anything, and it helps me feel less nervous."

Own Our Past

"I've had a tough couple of years, and it's affected us both. I've pushed you away, and my drinking has gotten worse."

Epiphany

"Recently, things got really dark for me, and I've decided that I need to get help for my PTSD."

Ask For Buy-In/Manage Expectations

"I have some ideas for getting help, and I know it will not be easy. I believe that with your support, I can start this fight."

Love Them

"I realize that I've put you through a lot. The most important thing I want you to know is that I love you, I love us, and I will do whatever it takes to make this work."

Be Silent

Seriously, do whatever it takes to be silent and let your partner speak next.

EXAMPLE 2
AGE APPROPRIATE

Ask Permission

"Hey buddy! I have something important I want to talk to you about, if that's okay. You're not in any trouble, don't worry. I want to talk to you a little about what I've been going through. Would that be okay?"

(STOP - wait for an answer.)

Introduce Our Elephant

"I realize that I'm crying a little, but I'm okay. Sometimes I feel so much love for you and Dad that it fills my heart and comes out of my eyeballs, and I promise you I'm okay."

Own Our Past

"I know that we haven't been spending as much time together as we used to, and that's my fault. I was too embarrassed to tell you, but sometimes I feel scared in crowds. Sometimes, I get really angry unexpectedly, too, and it scares me."

Epiphany

"Even though I feel scared sometimes, I've decided that I want to be the best Mommy I can be, so I'm going to work on facing my fears with the help of a therapist. That's a special kind of mind doctor."

Ask For Buy-In/Manage Expectations

"This means that I'll be going to see the doctor a lot over the next few weeks. They are going to give me lots of homework assignments. I might seem grumpy, but that doesn't mean I'm grumpy with you. If I do everything the doctor asks, I'll work through all of my grumpys. And I'm hoping you might help too, with some encouragement to keep me motivated."

Love Them

"I imagine it feels scary to see me acting angry, and it scares me too. I imagine you feel pretty lonely when I'm in one of those cranky moods. And that is why I have to get better. You are so important to me. I need you to know that. I love you. You can talk to me about any feelings you have, and I will do my best to answer all of your questions. I want to be there for you, too."

Be Silent

Be silent and let your child speak next.

EXAMPLE 3

Ask Permission

"Mom/Dad, I'm glad we have a chance to talk, even if it's just on the phone. I know you've been worried about me, and the truth is that I've been worried about me, too. I want to tell you what I've been going through and I'll need about 30 seconds to get it all out. After that, I promise I'll answer any questions you have. Would that be okay?"

(STOP - wait for an answer.)

Introduce Our Elephant

"It's hard for me to connect with my feelings, so while it may sound like I'm numb or like I don't feel anything, I promise you that I do and I'm okay."

Own Our Past

"I've had a tough time getting back to my normal life since the divorce. I stopped calling you weekly like I used to because I didn't want you to worry about me, but I realize that probably made you worry more."

Epiphany

"I've been talking to some friends and I've decided I want to get help."

Ask For Buy-In/Manage Expectations

"I'll be looking into getting professional help and I could use a weekly check-in again. I realize that I'm the one who stopped calling you, and I'm sorry I did that. I really miss talking to you every week."

Love Them

"I can't imagine what it was like for you not to hear from me, and I'm so sorry. I want you to know that I love you, and I'm so thankful you are my Mom/Dad."

Be Silent

Be silent and let them speak next.

These conversations are hard, but not having social support is infinitely harder. Also, what do we really have to lose here? Nothing, and we have everything to gain by connecting or reconnecting with the people who love us.

CHAPTER 12 PTSD AND WORK

In the last chapter, we discussed how to talk to those people in our lives who deserve our narratives; those who support us and love us. In this chapter, we're going to talk about folks who don't. It's likely that you work with them.

Before you get offended and write a strongly worded email, We're happy for you if you are the exception and have a workplace that feels like one big happy family. The rest of us live in Realityville with crappy bosses, catty co-workers, and faceless HR departments.

> *Here's the deal: unless we are independently wealthy, before and after we get PTSD treatment we have to go back to work.*

Like our loved ones, everyone in the office knows we need help. Unlike our loved ones, they can be judgy, passive-aggressive, small-talkity, single-minded jerks who take glee in seeing us fail.

But we digress.

Here's the Bottom-Line Up Front:

> ## We either control the narrative,
> ## or the narrative controls us.

In order to reintegrate back into the workplace after getting treatment, or get support from our workplace to go out and get treatment, we have to talk to our bosses and our colleagues about our PTSD. It's not fair, and it's none of their business. We hear you. But that's life.

This chapter is going to teach us how to control our narrative, and get buy-in and support from our workplace, so we can get back to doing our job.

THERE IS A NARRATIVE, AND THERE IS AN ELEPHANT

Let's be clear: there are no secrets in the workplace. When we have issues, especially mental health issues, everybody knows about it. That's not to say that what they know is accurate, but everybody knows something is up. When we make the decision not to talk about our treatment (or need for treatment), an elephant is born.

We're going to speak plainly here: choosing to ignore our PTSD or avoid talking about it at work is not realistic. We can be ten types of brilliant, but our colleagues are thinking, "Are we really not going to talk about her being in the hospital for four weeks?" or, "Are we just going to pretend she never had a panic attack in the bathroom?"

We have to address it. It's not fair. We know.

CONTROL THE NARRATIVE

How can we talk to our bosses and our colleagues about our PTSD in a way that (1) controls the narrative, and (2) gets us buy-in and possible social support (even if only superficial) so that we can get the help we need?

We are going to create an elevator speech similar to the one from the last chapter. But, unlike talking with our loved ones, this elevator speech uses our narrative to advocate for our needs:

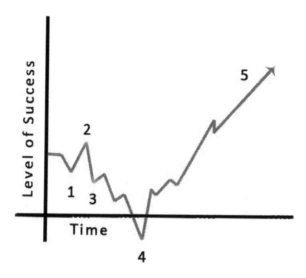

Leaning on our inspirational narrative model, this elevator speech will be tightened up and acknowledge the formality of a work setting.

This elevator speech for the workplace has 6 parts:

1. Thank them for opportunity to talk.
2. Introduce our elephant - own emotion/lack of emotion.
3. Own our past - own our narrative, speak plainly.
4. Turning point – epiphany.
5. Ask for buy-in, manage expectations.
6. Thank them, show dedication.

1. Thank them for the opportunity to talk.

When talking with HR, or anyone within our workplace chain of command, we don't always have the luxury of asking for uninterrupted time to talk. So, we'll start by thanking them for taking the time to speak with us (even if no one had a choice).

If possible, proactively ask for an opportunity to speak with the boss or HR department. This shows courage, controls the narrative, and proves how serious we are about our treatment and recovery.

2. Introduce our elephant.

We remember that whenever our elephant is in the room, we will introduce it. Again, feeling nervous, emotional, frustrated, or numb is okay. Using a note card is okay, just introduce it. It may sound like this: "In order to respect your time, I took some notes to help me stay on point" or, "It is nerve-racking to speak to you about my PTSD because of the stigma, so I thank you for your patience."

3. Own our past.

This is still an opportunity for us to own our behavior and not make any excuses. Focus on work issues and speak in concise terms. Again, no new revelations. We do not have to share details of our trauma with our bosses and colleagues; keep it simple.

4. The epiphany.

Again, this is our "a-ha!" moment when we make the choice to change. What was it that brought us to this point? This can sound like, "After the police picked me up, I realized that my life had spiraled out of control and I know I need help."

5. Ask for buy-in, manage expectations.

This is why we're here: we need support from our bosses and colleagues so we can get the help we need. It is also the time for us to manage expectations: this journey is not going to be easy, and we are dedicated to trying. It may sound something like, "I want to recover from PTSD, and I know it's not easy. I'll need to attend counseling weekly and take time off from work. I believe that with your continued support, I can do this."

Notice the word "continued" here. We are smart to use some sugar when dealing with upper management.

6. Thank them/show dedication.

Again, even if our bosses and colleagues are sub-par, it doesn't hurt to thank them.

When it comes to showing dedication, we get to be dedicated to whatever we want to be dedicated to; just speak plainly and get to the point: "Thank you for giving me an opportunity to talk to you today. I want you to know that I'm dedicated to our team and to our mission."

We can be dedicated to finishing out a drug treatment program, or dedicated to taking good care of our family.

SOME EXAMPLES

As with the previous chapter, we want to take an opportunity to give some examples of elevator speeches to help you feel confident in formulating your own. The level of formality will depend on your workplace chain of command and your boss's personalities.

EXAMPLE 1

Thank Them

"Sir, thank you for giving me the opportunity to speak to you today."

Introduce Our Elephant

"I apologize if I sound a bit nervous. I am, and I made some notes to help me stay on point in respect of your time."

Own Our Past

"I've been struggling lately and it has affected my work and attendance. I tried working things out on my own and found I needed more help."

Epiphany

"I reached out to EAP and they found me professional help and resources to focus on getting better. So far it is having a positive impact."

Ask For Buy-In

"My doctor recommended that I attend weekly appointments over the next couple months and my goal is to follow my doctor's guidance closely and get to a place where I am stronger. I would very much appreciate your support in this."

Thank Them/Show Dedication

"Sir, thank you for allowing me the time to speak with you today. I want you to know that I'm dedicated to this company and my work team and I am thankful for your time and attention to my request."

EXAMPLE 2

Thank Them

"Ma'am, I'd like to thank you and our work team for giving me an opportunity to address you today."

Introduce Our Elephant

"I feel nervous talking to the team because I worry you may not be able to relate to my military service."

Own Our Past

"Since I got out of the military, adjusting to civilian life was not as easy as I thought it would be. I've had problems connecting with people at work, and I've struggled in personal ways."

Epiphany

"Recently, a buddy of mine committed suicide, and it was hard. I went to see a counselor, and I found out I have PTSD."

Ask For Buy-In

"I realize that there's a lot of stigma about PTSD, and I'm lucky to have a team that is supportive. I believe that with your continued support, I can make a full recovery."

Thank Them/Show Dedication

"Thank you for taking the time to hear me out. I want you to know that I'm dedicated to this company, to this team, and to our project."

The goal of an elevator speech in the workplace is to (1) control the narrative, and (2) get buy-in and possible social support from bosses and colleagues. The first will minimize drama and the second will push us forward toward recovery. It works.

CHAPTER 13 RELAPSE PREVENTION

After we get help with our PTSD, we have to think about relapse. We tend to associate relapse with drug or alcohol use, but this simply means a period of deterioration after a period of improvement.

This can happen with PTSD, depression, anxiety, or pretty much anything relating to our health (mental or physical).

> *Relapse happens,*
> *and it's not the end of the world.*

One of the chief components of a good relapse prevention plan is to increase self-awareness and be aware of your behaviors and thoughts.

This is key because recognizing what triggers a relapse, and catching yourself in negative thoughts or behaviors, is step one in your plan to get back on back on track.

WHAT ARE YOUR WARNING SIGNS?

These can be things, such as the experience of certain emotions, changes in thoughts, or changes in behavior. You may run into a reminder of your trauma or get pulled into a conversation about something that reminds you of it.

Anniversaries of a traumatic event are also unavoidable and are often associated with a resurgence in PTSD symptoms.

Pay special attention to sudden changes in mood or thoughts like:

"No one cares about me or what I do. What's the point of going on?"

"I can't stand being around anyone!"

"Maybe a drink or two will take the edge off my feelings for a little while."

"I don't remember the last time I showered. I don't have the energy to do anything these days."

"Therapy is a waste of time."

Awareness of your warning signs will allow you to catch yourself and implement coping strategies you learned during treatment. Recognition is step one towards stopping these PTSD symptoms before they have a chance to become unmanageable. If you need to, this would also be a good time to check in with your therapist.

SETTING BOUNDARIES AT WORK AND IN LIFE

For many people, strong social support fosters recovery, and toxic relationships usher in relapse. To manage the latter, we need to talk about boundaries.

Boundaries protect you. They let the people around you know how you define what is acceptable or unacceptable. For people who have been through traumatic experiences, however, this task is a tough one.

Experiencing trauma makes you feel unsafe, and can challenge your sense of self-worth, which can lead you, and other trauma survivors to lean back on placating or maladaptive tendencies in order to avoid conflict.

See if any of these sound familiar.

- **Can't Say "No"**

  You've had to use "Yes" to avoid conflict with a parental figure, bully, or some other figure of authority. Saying "no" has always been met with more stress, guilt, or drama than it is worth, so it has become your default answer.

- **People Pleasing**

  You go along to get along. You've been through a nightmare and see no need to provoke anything else. At least, that's how it feels when you don't put the needs of others first. Left unchecked, this trend can get to the point where you have trouble even identifying your own needs.

- **Lack of Trust**

  A person, or people, who you've relied on for safety or protection, was the cause of your trauma, which has eroded your systems of trust. As a result, you no longer trust anyone. So why bother setting boundaries when they will just be ignored or disrespected anyway, right?

In short; to keep the peace, trauma survivors tend to not put their needs first.

That has to change.

Setting healthy boundaries is an essential part of recovery.

Often, trauma survivors will feel like they don't deserve to be respected or valued. Boundaries are especially important here because the act of setting them, and holding that line, challenge the negative opinions trauma survivors have about themselves. They are an act of self-love that not only protects the survivor from others, they also work to reinforce the survivors' reemerging sense of self-worth.

Healthy boundaries are the ultimate form of self-respect. They say to us and the world, "I deserve to be honored, respected, and valued." Boundaries denote confidence. Since confidence is often one of the casualties of PTSD, we have to relearn (or maybe learn for the first time) how to make a healthy, reasonable boundary, how to maintain it, and what to do if someone chooses to ignore it.

Truth Bomb: Bullying

When we are going through a hard time, we are much more likely to be bullied. Bullies seek out and prey on targets, aiming their venom at those they consider vulnerable or socially isolated. Our PTSD symptoms set us up to be targets, especially criteria C (avoidance) and D (negative alterations in cognition and mood). Also, our arousal symptoms (criterion E) may have put us on the radar because of an angry outburst or reckless behavior. Healthy boundaries curtail bullying because we stop playing the game.

If we find that we are being bullied, we can learn more about the psychology behind it so that we can (1) understand that the problem isn't us, (2) create a strong social support system, and (3) make a plan to change the situation. *The Bully at Work* and *The Asshole Survival Guide* are books I recommend.

Making healthy boundaries seems like it should be easy and intuitive, but it's not.

Let's start here:

GROUND RULES

1. Healthy boundaries make healthy relationships.

There is no such thing as a healthy relationship without boundaries, whether it is a marriage relationship, a friend, colleagues, or the relationship you have with your children. Healthy boundaries say, "I deserve to be honored, respected, and valued" and this is important for any healthy interpersonal relationship.

2. People do not know our boundaries unless we state them clearly and succinctly.

Yes, in a perfect world, people "should" know how to act, but suffice it to say that not everyone is great at adulting. Some people do not know that racist comments are not okay. Some people do not understand that unsolicited touching is creepy. Let's not waste time getting mad about what "should be." Instead, let's remember that half the people we meet are below average and common sense is not common. Boundaries are not intuitive. We must state our boundaries clearly and concisely—out loud—to other people.

3. Reasonable people respect reasonable boundaries.

The inherent problem with this is that not all people are reasonable. Sad news of the day: the world is full of psychopaths and assholes. When people choose to ignore reasonable boundaries, they are sometimes the former and usually the latter. The problem is not our boundary, it is their *choice*.

4. Our boundaries, their choice.

We create healthy boundaries, and we have absolutely no control over other people or how they act. When we state our healthy boundaries—out loud—clearly and concisely, other people then *choose* whether they want to respect our boundaries or not.

> *When people choose to ignore our reasonable boundaries, they are saying in no uncertain terms, loud and clear: "I do not respect you and I do not want a relationship with you that is not on my terms." No exceptions.*

THE HOW-TO

When making a healthy boundary, we want to be sure it is reasonable, clear, and direct. We suggest using this model:

"I don't like it when you ___. Please stop."

Fill in the blank. Here are some examples:

"I don't like it when you stare. Please stop."

"That word is offensive. Please don't use it."

"I don't like hugging people. Can we fist bump?"

What we like about this model is that it is not attacking the person; it addresses behavior. It is also short and to the point.

We remember that this must be a reasonable boundary.

We're not saying, *"I don't like it when you breathe, please stop,"* but we are making a legitimate, healthy boundary.

PUSH-BACK

Let's restate: reasonable people respect reasonable boundaries. When we cross a boundary and someone lets us know, our only reasonable response is, "I'm sorry; it won't happen again." We made a mistake and now we know, going forward. It's nothing personal. End of story.

Not everyone is reasonable, and we'll probably experience push-back from time to time. This will range from a surprised, "you never said anything before," to an accusatory, "no one else seems to have a problem with it," to a full out obnoxious tantrum of, "this is who I am, and I don't have to change 'cause I don't wanna!"

Our course of action is to **simply and calmly restate our boundaries.**

Here are some examples:

"I hear you. I still find that word offensive. Please stop using it."

"It's not personal. I just don't like hugging."

"No one is trying to hurt your feelings or make you feel sad on the inside. Please stop."

Sometimes, the push-back gets personal and downright ugly, especially if someone feels they deserve to act however they want. Let's remember that being a jerk is their choice, and that they are choosing to say, "I don't think that you deserve to be honored, respected, or valued."

The message is loud and clear, so listen.

> "When someone shows you who they are,
> believe them the first time."
> Maya Angelou

IN ACTION

We swear a lot. Some people don't like it. Let's say that you are one of our students and you approach after class and say, "I don't like it when you swear. Please stop."

You know what will happen?

We'll apologize and sincerely do our best to stop swearing in front of you. We may slip up, but we will sincerely try.

The reason is simple: ***We value our relationship with our students more than the need to swear.*** We will choose to respect your boundary because we believe that everyone deserves to be honored, respected, and valued. End of story.

Not everyone values their relationships with us more than they value their need to violate perfectly reasonable boundaries.

When this happens, we can't change the person - so we may have to change the relationship.

But I Want to be Liked/Loved

Not everyone will like us, and that is okay.

Furthermore, not everyone who "should" love us chooses to act in a way that honors, values, and respects us.

When we make a boundary, others make a choice, and it is our responsibility to respect that choice - even if it means that the other person chooses to no longer be in a relationship with us.

It is tempting to get caught up in the "shoulds," as in "my parent 'should' love me," or "my spouse 'should' respect me." We urge everyone to collectively stop *should-ing* all over ourselves. Family members know how to push our buttons because they installed them.

Rejection hurts, but not as much as chasing the love of someone who has very clearly said that they choose not to honor, value, or respect us.

QUICK LIST

We've introduced a lot in this chapter, so we want to wrap it up with some quick tips for creating and maintaining healthy boundaries:

- Give ourselves permission. Everyone deserves to feel honored, respected, and valued - even us.
- Name our limits. Take time to decide for ourselves what behavior is and is not okay. If you wouldn't treat a friend that way, don't allow yourself to be treated that way.
- Practice self-awareness. If someone's behavior feels creepy or uncomfortable, this is probably a boundary.
- Be direct. We don't have to explain our reasons for having reasonable boundaries. Unreasonable people don't care anyway and are just being manipulative.
- Seek support. Social support is an important part of self-care. A therapist can be an excellent sounding board and provide good insight. So can a support group, church, and good friends.

Start small. Like any new skill, creating healthy boundaries takes practice. We can start with a small boundary that isn't too threatening and then increase to more challenging boundaries.

Learning how to create and maintain healthy boundaries will support our PTSD recovery and help us to regain confidence and self-respect.

FINAL NOTE

We wrote this book for you because we've been there before and know how to get out. Now we want you to recover, because you deserve it.

We've covered a lot: what PTSD is and isn't, Moral Injury, what treatments work, how to find treatment and social support, how to talk to others about our PTSD, and how to protect our recovery through healthy boundaries.

Our hope is that you have a lot more tools now than when you started.

Since you've stuck with us until the end, we'll leave you with this piece. Full disclosure, it is military-based, but the underlying message is one we think translates universally to those who are struggling with PTSD.

A Soldier with PTSD fell into a hole and couldn't get out. A Senior NCO went by and the Soldier with PTSD called out for help. The Senior NCO yelled, told him to suck it up, dig deep, and drive on, then threw him a shovel. But the Soldier with PTSD could not suck it up and drive on so he dug the hole deeper.

A Senior Officer went by and the Soldier with PTSD called out for help. The Senior Officer told him to use the tools his Senior NCO gave him and then threw him a bucket. But the Soldier with PTSD was using the tools his Senior NCO gave him, so he dug the hole deeper and filled the bucket.

A psychiatrist walked by. The Soldier with PTSD said, "Help! I can't get out!" The psychiatrist gave him some drugs and said, "Take this. It will relieve the pain." The Soldier with PTSD said thanks, but when the pills ran out, he was still in the hole.

A well-known psychologist rode by and heard the Soldier with PTSD crying for help. He stopped and asked, "How did you get there? Were you born there? Did your parents put you there? Tell me about yourself, it will alleviate your sense of loneliness." So, the Soldier with PTSD talked with him for an hour, then the psychologist had to leave, but he said he'd be back next week. The Soldier with PTSD thanked him, but he was still in the hole.

A priest came by. The Soldier with PTSD called for help. The priest gave him a Bible and said, "I'll say a prayer for you." He got down on his knees and prayed for the Soldier with PTSD, then he left. The Soldier with PTSD was very grateful, he read the Bible, but he was still stuck in the hole.

A recovering Soldier with PTSD happened to be passing by. The Soldier with PTSD cried out, "Hey, help me. I'm stuck in this hole!" Right away the recovering Soldier with PTSD jumped down in the hole with him. The Soldier with PTSD said, "What are you doing? Now we're both stuck here!" But the recovering Soldier with PTSD said, "Calm down. It's okay. I've been here before. I know how to get out."

-Author Unknown

LINKS AND RESOURCES

National Suicide Prevention Lifeline
https://suicidepreventionlifeline.org/
(800) 273-8255

Nacional de Prevención del Suicidio
(888) 628-9454

National Suicide Prevention Lifeline (Options for Deaf and Hard of Hearing)
For TTY Users: Use your preferred relay service or dial 711 then 1-800-273-8255

The American Foundation for Suicide Prevention provides referrals to support groups and mental health professionals, resources on loss, and suicide prevention information (888-333-2377)
https://afsp.org/

Crisis Text Line
https://www.crisistextline.org/
Text HOME to 741741

National Domestic Violence Hotline
https://www.thehotline.org/
(800) 799-7233

Veterans Crisis Line
https://www.veteranscrisisline.net/
(800) 273-8255, PRESS 1 or
Text 838255

National Grad Crisis Line
https://gradresources.org/crisis/
(877) 472-3457

National Sexual Assault Hotline
https://www.rainn.org/resources
(800) 656-4673

Childhelp National Child Abuse Hotline
https://www.childhelp.org/hotline-impact-reports/
(800) 422-4453 – Call or Text

Substance Abuse and Mental Health Services Administration National Helpline
https://www.samhsa.gov/find-help/national-helpline
(800) 662-4357 or TTY – 1-800-487-4889

National Alliance on Mental Illness
https://nami.org/Home
1-800-950-6264

Alcoholics Anonymous
https://www.aa.org/

Narcotics Anonymous
https://na.org/

Sidran Institute
https://www.sidran.org/
helps people understand, manage, and treat trauma and dissociation; maintains a helpline for information and referrals
(410-825-8888)

Anxiety and Depression Association of America (ADAA)
https://adaa.org/
provides information on prevention, treatment and symptoms of anxiety, depression and related conditions
(240-485-1001)

National Estimates of Exposure to Traumatic Events and PTSD Prevalence Using DSM-IV and DSM-5 Criteria
https://www.ncbi.nlm.nih.gov/pmc/articles/PMC4096796/
Suicide: The Forever Decision by Paul G. Quinnett, PhD.

Moral Injury by Brett Litz
https://www.sciencedirect.com/science/article/pii/S0272735809000920?via%3Dihub

Transgressive Acts A Review of Research on Moral Injury in Combat Veterans
http://dx.doi.org/10.1037/mil0000132

In describing the difference between guilt and shame, by Brené Brown
https://www.ted.com/talks/brene_brown_listening_to_shame?language=en

On Killing: The Psychological Cost of Learning to Kill in War and Society by Lt. Col. Dave Grossman
https://en.wikipedia.org/wiki/On_Killing

STRONG STAR is focused on reducing the suffering of our nation's wounded warriors and first responders.
http://www.strongstar.org/

EMDR Institute
www.emdr.com

Nidal Hassan / Confidentiality
https://www.nytimes.com/2013/08/21/us/fort-hood-gunman-nidal-malik-hasan.html

Certified Group Psychotherapist
http://member.agpa.org/imis/agpa/cgpdirectory/cgpdirectory.aspx

Does asking about suicide and related behaviours induce suicidal ideation? What is the evidence?
https://www.ncbi.nlm.nih.gov/pubmed/24998511

To find a PTSD specialist, we can get help from Military One Source
https://www.militaryonesource.mil/confidential-help

How to Find the Best Therapist for You
https://www.psychologytoday.com/us/blog/freudian-sip/201102/how-find-the-best-therapist-you

The importance of social support in treating PTSD
Relations between Social Support, PTSD Symptoms, and Substance Use in Veterans
https://www.ncbi.nlm.nih.gov/pmc/articles/PMC5507582/

Support groups
https://suicidology.org/resources/support-groups/

Harvard professor, Robert Rosenthal experiment
Teachers' Expectations Can Influence How Students Perform
https://www.npr.org/sections/health-shots/2012/09/18/161159263/teachers-expectations-can-influence-how-students-perform

About Prolonged Exposure Therapy
https://www.med.upenn.edu/ctsa/workshops_pet.html

About Cognitive Processing Therapy
https://cptforptsd.com/

About Eye Movement Desensitization and Reprocessing
https://www.emdr.com/what-is-emdr/

Take The ACE Quiz
https://www.npr.org/sections/health-shots/2015/03/02/387007941/take-the-ace-quiz-and-learn-what-it-does-and-doesnt-mean
Please note, this sample quiz is not a replacement for an actual therapeutic assessment. It does, however, provide some good background information.

VOCABULARY QUICK REFERENCE

Ladies, we absolutely have to know our symptoms better than anyone else – this includes our doctors and/or our therapists. This book has been a heavy read, and we don't want you to have to search for the simple stuff. Use this section as a quick reference guide to help you locate the exact term you need.

Acceptance and Commitment Therapy (ACT): A form of Mindfulness-Based Cognitive Therapy that seeks to develop psychological flexibility and encourages people to embrace their thoughts and feelings rather than fighting or feeling guilty for them.

Acute Stress Disorder (ASD): Is the continuing and extreme traumatic stress response that significantly interferes with daily life in the month following the traumatic exposure.

Acute Trauma: exposure to a single traumatic event.

Adaptive Disclosure: Prolonged Exposure Therapy is supplemented with various perspective taking interventions involving imaginal dialogues with a "moral authority" who judges, but also has the authority to forgive the person for their breach of morality or ethics.

Adverse Childhood Experience (ACE): The types of abuse, neglect, or other potentially traumatic experiences that can happen to a person under the age of 18. These potentially traumatic events can have negative, lasting effects on a person's development, the way they interact with others, and how they perform in school.

Avoidance: The DSM defines this as avoiding internal things (like memories, thoughts, or feelings) or avoiding external things (like people, places, and things that remind us of the trauma).

Betrayal Blindness: A term used to describe an unwillingness to recognize abuse that is ongoing.

Bilateral Stimulation (BLS): consists of alternating right and left stimulation, whether it's tapping of the toes or tapping on the shoulders. It can also include audio or visual stimulation with the use of light. This stimulation may include eye movements, taps, or tones.

Borderline Personality Disorder (BPD): Is a mental illness that severely impacts a person's ability to regulate their emotions. This loss of emotional control can increase impulsivity, affect how a person feels about themselves, and negatively impact their relationships with others.

Body Scan: In EMDR therapy, this is the step where the client recognizes changes in their body sensations when thinking of negative triggers. It can reveal tension points to triggers that still need to be targeted by the therapist for additional processing.

Bullying: Is aggressive behavior, often seen among school-aged children (but can also happen during adulthood), that involves inflicting of social, emotional, physical, and/or psychological harm to someone who often is perceived as being less powerful.

Social bullying: involves hurting someone's reputation or relationships and includes in person and online interactions.

Physical bullying: involves hurting a person or their possessions.

Verbal bullying: includes teasing, name-calling, inappropriate sexual comments, taunting, and threatening to cause harm.

Cyberbullying: Is a modern form of bullying using the internet, social media, or smartphones.

Burnout (BO): The consequences of severe stress and high ideals in "helping" professions. It is a syndrome resulting from chronic workplace stress that has not been successfully managed.

Childhood Sexual Abuse—As defined by the 1999 WHO Consultation on Child Abuse Prevention: *Child sexual abuse is the involvement of a child in sexual activity that he or she does not fully comprehend, is unable to give informed consent to, or for which the child is not developmentally prepared and cannot give consent, or that violates the laws or social taboos of society.*

Cognitive Processing Therapy (CPT): includes impact statements and workbook exercises used to identify and address unhelpful thinking patterns related to safety, trust, power and control, esteem, and intimacy. Our therapist will ask questions and work with us to recognize unhelpful thinking patterns, reframe our thoughts, reduce our symptoms, and come to a better understanding about ourselves and our relationships.

Compassion Fatigue: refers to a set of negative psychological symptoms that caregivers experience in the course of their work while being exposed to direct traumatic events or through secondary trauma.

Complex PTSD (C-PTSD): The C- distinction reflects the complexity of issues that develop due to the repetitive nature of the trauma experienced over a long period of time. Often stemming from childhood, the extended duration of traumatic experiences often necessitates an altered and longer approach to treatment, emotional regulation skill building to overcome learned behaviors and habits that formed as coping mechanisms, and a somatic level of work to help retrain the nervous system to function and respond appropriately instead of defaulting to stress responses.

Chronic Trauma: ongoing or prolonged exposure to traumatic stress or traumatic events.

Cognitive Labor: The care work (See, Mental Load) outside of the workplace.

Complex Trauma: exposure to multiple forms of trauma or traumatic events.

Consent: A freely given agreement to the conduct at issue by a competent person.

Co-Occurring Disorders: when we are diagnosed with two or more simultaneously occurring conditions. This is unbelievably common with PTSD. For example, we'll have PTSD and a substance or alcohol abuse problem at the same time, or PTSD and depression. The most common co-occurring disorders seen with PTSD are anxiety, depression, drug/alcohol misuse, eating disorders, and OCD.

Desensitization: A treatment or process that diminishes emotional responsiveness to a negative, aversive, or positive stimulus after repeated exposure to it.

Diagnostic and Statistical Manual, Version Five (DSM-5): Is a big purple book that should be on our therapist's bookshelf. Version five came out in 2013 and changed the definition of PTSD.

Dissociation: A 50-cent word that means disconnection.

Domestic Abuse: also known as Domestic Violence or Intimate Partner Violence, is a behavioral pattern rooted in dominance that is used to gain or maintain control over a partner.

Economic Abuse: Restricting access to job and money, making a person reliant on the abuser.

Emotional Abuse: Using insults, shame, and isolation to undermine a person's self-worth and take away their agency. In general, a relationship is emotionally abusive when there is a consistent pattern of abusive words and bullying behaviors that wear down a person's self-esteem and undermine their mental health.

Emotional Labor: The process of managing feelings and expressions to fulfill the emotional requirements of a job. Emotional work done in a paid work setting. Often gendered, considered to be women's work, part of an ongoing history of care-taking labor where mostly marginalized people are expected to give their energy, time, and emotional capacity to serve others.

Emotional Dysregulation: describes an emotional response that is poorly regulated and does not fall within the traditionally accepted range of emotional reaction. It may also be referred to as marked fluctuation or a mood swing.

Emotional Regulation: The ability to exert control over one's own emotional state. It may involve behaviors such as re-thinking a challenging situation to reduce anger or anxiety, hiding visible signs of sadness or fear, or focusing on reasons to feel happy or calm.

Emotion Work: The social tasks one performs to satisfy others. Unpaid emotional work that a person undertakes in their private life.

Evidence-based treatment (EBTs): Treatments that have been peer-reviewed with substantial and verifiable scientific evidence to prove they work most of the time, for most people.

Eye-Movement Desensitization and Reprocessing (EMDR): an eight-phase treatment that focuses attention on three distinct time periods: the past, present, and future while engaging in Bilateral Stimulation (BLS) to help replace the negative memory or thought with positive ones. It is believed that BLS activates both hemispheres of the brain, which can have a soothing effect, by dimming the intensity of the memory while allowing the client space to process it without an overwhelming psychological response.

Gaslighting: Is a way of invalidating through persistent undermining, another person's reality by denying facts, the environment around them, or their feelings.

Guilt: A negative feeling related to a particular action.

Habituation: in PE Therapy, this is a decrease in response to a stimulus after repeated presentations.

Impact Statement: In CPT, this is a detailed account of your traumatic experience, including sensory details that you remember. This process of writing it out, allows exploration of the thoughts and beliefs about the trauma.

Institutional Betrayal: wrongdoings perpetrated by an institution upon individuals who depend on that institution. This includes any failure to prevent or appropriately respond to wrongdoings perpetrated by members of, or within, the institution.

Intergenerational Trauma: The passing down of trauma through generations. Exposure to extremely adverse events in childhood can affect an individual so much that their offspring are affected by their parents' post-traumatic state. While this was initially identified among children of Holocaust survivors, it applies to child abuse survivors, too.

Intermittent Reinforcement: when our brains are randomly rewarded at varying, unpredictable times, we continue to seek those rewards, like an addict, even if there will never be another.

Intimidation: creating fear by using looks, actions, gestures, a loud voice, smashing things, or destroying property.

Intrusion Symptoms: unwanted and involuntary intrusive symptoms of PTSD that include; distressing thoughts, images, or memories; flashbacks or disassociation; nightmares, distressing reminders of our trauma; and body cues.

LGBTQI+: Lesbian, gay, bisexual, transgender, queer, intersex, non-binary or otherwise gender non-conforming. In other words, children that exist outside of primary cisgender identities.

Marital / Spousal Rape: The act of sexual intercourse with one's spouse without the spouse's consent. The lack of consent is the essential element and need not involve physical violence. Marital / Spousal Rape is considered a form of domestic violence and sexual abuse.

Medical Gaslighting Is when a medical professional downplays or dismisses what a patient is telling them. This can be traumatic and abusive.

Medical Trauma: A set of psychological and physiological responses to pain, injury, serious illness, medical procedures, and frightening treatment experiences.

Mental load: The primary component of this is that one person is handling the majority of the work required to maintain a relationship or care for another individual, while others are oblivious to the work being done and/or are unwilling to help with that work.

Minimizing: using Gaslighting techniques to create blame shifting so the abuser appears innocent while the survivor appears crazy.

Moral Injury: Perpetrating, failing to prevent, or bearing witness to acts that transgress deeply held moral beliefs and expectations.

Narcissistic Personality Disorder (NPD): A psychological personality disorder, defined by The DSM-5, characterized by an inflated sense of one's own importance, a deep need for excessive attention and admiration, troubled relationships, and a lack of empathy for others.

Narcissistic Rage: refers to the tendency for people with NPD to fly into a powerful outburst that can include anger, aggression, and violence, often with only the slightest provocation. This rage is child-like in nature and goes straight from the feeling of stress to a full-blown explosive reaction.

Post-Traumatic Stress Disorder (PTSD): The result of exposure to trauma, where the symptoms of that trauma persist or get worse in the weeks and months after the traumatic event.

Prolonged Exposure Therapy (PE): utilizes a technique called "imaginal exposure." After learning breathing techniques to manage anxiety, we imagine and describe the traumatic event in detail with guidance from a therapist. After the imaginal exposure, we process the experience with our therapist. Sessions are recorded on audio to listen to between sessions; this helps us to further process our emotions and practice breathing techniques.

Rape (FBI revised definition): Penetration, no matter how slight, of the vagina or anus with any body part or object, or oral penetration by a sex organ of another person, without consent.

Relational Aggression: This type of bullying includes verbal assaults, ostracizing, spreading rumors, and gossiping. The ability to disguise actions through passive-aggressive behavior, makes this type of bullying more difficult to spot.

Relational Trauma: An aftereffect of abuse, neglect, and suffering where the trauma survivor's ability to forge healthy connections with others has been altered by intense betrayal.

Secondary Traumatic Stress (STS): Is the stress resulting from helping or wanting to help a traumatized or suffering person.

Sexting—sending or receiving sexually explicit messages or images between electronic devices.

Sexual Assault / Abuse: refers to a range of unwanted behavior, coercion, and forceful sexual contact. This includes rape, attempted rape, and or unwanted physical contact.

Sexual Coercion: Is when someone manipulates you into unwanted sexual activity through non-physical means.

Shame: A feeling of diminished self-worth that is not related to any particular action.

Social Trauma: Social pressure, exclusion, humiliation, or rejection that results in symptoms of social anxiety disorder.

Somatic Therapy / Work: somatic means "relating to the body." Somatic psychotherapy is an umbrella term for therapies that center on the mind-body connection.

Threats: Making threats to do something to hurt a person emotionally or physically.

Toxic Shame: A deep and debilitating pathology that results from traumatic experiences of being repeatedly humiliated, rejected, despised, and treated as worthless.

Toxic Positivity: A form of invalidation that falls into the family of Gaslighting (See Emotional Abuse). Instead of facing difficult emotions, Toxic Positivity rejects or ignores the negative in favor of a cheerful, often falsely positive, facade.

Traumatic Bonds: Emotional attachment, known as a Trauma Bond, develops out of a repeated cycle of abuse, devaluation, and positive reinforcement.

Traumatic Stress (TS): Is the response to a traumatic event. It is a normal reaction to a terrible event, but symptoms usually get better over time.

Treatment-Resistant PTSD (TR-PTSD): An individual who, despite adequate treatment with antidepressants and cognitive behavioral therapy, still meets the criteria for PTSD is considered treatment-resistant. Resistance to PTSD treatment can be associated with more severe cases of PTSD, the experience of multiple traumas, the type of trauma, or other co-occuring psychiatric disorders and gender-related issues.

Trigger: memories, objects, people, etc. that spark intense negative emotions.

Vicarious Trauma: A theoretical term that focuses on the profound negative changes in a person's worldview due to the exposure to traumatic content of the people they help.

ABOUT THE AUTHORS

VIRGINIA CRUSE

Virginia Cruse is a Licensed Professional Counselor and National Certified Counselor specializing in Military Issues and Combat-Related Trauma. She provides crisis intervention and Evidence-Based Treatments for Post-Traumatic Stress Disorder, Moral Injury, Depression, Combat Operational Stress, and other diagnoses.

Virginia is a certified clinician in Cognitive Processing Therapy and Prolonged Exposure Therapy and has 20+ years' experience serving Active Duty Military, Veterans, Military retirees, and family members. She is a Certified Group Psychotherapist (CGP) and active American Group Psychotherapy Association member.

Virginia is a former Reserve Officer, Combat Veteran, and published researcher. She has one amazing husband, Jay, and one terrible dog, Peanut.

Virginia practices in Texas and Louisiana.
Find out more at:
http://www.thesoldiersblog.com/

ABOUT THE AUTHORS

KATIE SALIDAS

Katie Salidas is a best-selling author of fiction and nonfiction, with more than thirty books published to date. Known for her unique genre-blending style, Salidas seamlessly bridges the gap between fantasy and reality. Since 2010 she's penned six unique Paranormal and Urban Fantasy book series. Her nonfiction offerings include, *Go Publish Yourself* and *Write (and Edit) the Damn Book.*

When she's not writing her books, Salidas is actively work-ing to help other authors in the pursuit of publishing as a consultant, educator, and ghostwriter with Rising Sign Books. As part of her efforts to help other authors succeed, Salidas produces and hosts the Spilling Ink Show podcast. Find out more about Katie Salidas by visiting her website.

Rising Sign Books
http://www.risingsignbooks.com/
Spilling Ink Show
https://www.youtube.com/c/SpillingInkShow
Amazon
https://www.amazon.com/Katie-Salidas/e/B003APXXWO

Your opinion matters!

When people first look at a book, beyond the description or cover, they pay close attention to what others, like you have to say. Reviews heavily influence that reader's decision to make a purchase.

You don't have to write a novel. That's our job!

Simply share what you thought of the book by answering two simple questions.

Was the information valuable?

Would you recommend it to someone else?

That's it!

Your opinion matters. It matters to us, because we want to ensure you are getting the most accurate and helpful information. And beyond our desire to educate you, the review you write could make (or break) the success of this book.

Made in the USA
Coppell, TX
28 June 2024

34027777R00153